Dag Hammarskjöld: A Spiritual Portrait

Courtesy of BLACK STAR (*photograph by* WERNER WOLFF)

Dag Hammarskjöld

A SPIRITUAL PORTRAIT

by Sven Stolpe

ENGLISH TRANSLATION BY NAOMI WALFORD

CHARLES SCRIBNER'S SONS, *New York*

In THIS book little will be said of Dag Hammarskjöld's public life and political achievements. To a great extent the documentary material is under seal, and it is still too early even to touch upon much of his private life or of his political work as Secretary-General of the United Nations.

Yet in his own book *Markings*, published posthumously in 1963, Dag Hammarskjöld himself emphasized his need to speak out in another context which he seems to have thought more important. In the preface, dedicated to Leif Belfrage, an eminent Swedish diplomat and close friend, he writes:

Dear Leif:

Perhaps you may remember I once told you that, in spite of everything, I kept a diary which I wanted you to take charge of some day.
Here it is.

It was begun without a thought of anybody else reading it. But, what with my later history and all that has been said and written about me, the situation has changed. These entries provide the only true "profile" that can be drawn. That is why, during recent years, I have reckoned with the possibility of publication, though I have continued to write for myself, not for the public.

If you find them worth publishing, you have my permission to do so—as a sort of *white book* concerning my negotiations with myself—and with God.

Dag

This little essay of mine is based not only on this diary but on letters and other material which I received personally from Hammarskjöld, with whom—though never one of his intimate friends —I was closely associated in youth, and in his latter years.

In this book I shall be concerned solely with Dag Hammarskjöld's spiritual journey: that is to say, with the spiritual and religious development that led him to what, in the culture of modern Sweden, is an almost unique example of Christian mysticism.

Sven Stolpe

Dag Hammarskjöld: A Spiritual Portrait

Chapter 1

DAG HAMMARSKJÖLD came of an old aristocratic Swedish family which for centuries had supplied the country with both civil servants and soldiers, many of whom attained high rank. The Hammarskjöld family traits are easily recognizable: seriousness, conscientiousness and dauntless energy. Whenever some knotty problem arises within the Swedish administration the response is likely to be: "Try one of the Hammarskjölds." Of Dag's brothers, Bo is one of the ablest government officials in Sweden, and a former lord-lieutenant of Nyköping. He has been described as the ideal official, able to prescribe ideal solutions to the toughest problems. Ake, another brother, was equally talented: he was Swedish envoy and Secretary-General to the International Court of Arbitration at The Hague (to which he was appointed at the age of 29), and member of a series of international conciliation committees during the hopeful years of the

League of Nations: the period described by Dag Hammarskjöld as "that strange, brief idyll that flourished all over Europe between two crises and two wars."

Brother Ake met an early death, being only 44 when he succumbed to a rheumatic illness. But the most eminent figure in the history of the Hammarskjöld family before Dag himself was his father, Hjalmar Hammarskjöld, Prime Minister, whom Dag so penetratingly portrayed in a speech to the Swedish Academy on the occasion —unique in the annals of that august body—of his succession as a member and as occupant of his father's chair.

Hjalmar Hammarskjöld was born in impoverished circumstances on an old family property in Småland: the province that has produced most of Sweden's more influential ruling families from the Middle Ages onwards. He was an exceptionally fine scholar with a special interest in the classical languages, and in his later years as emeritus he concentrated on Portuguese and South American lyric poetry on behalf of the Nobel Committee. He was an eminent connoisseur of classical German literature, and was particularly drawn to Platen—whom he liked to translate—and to Hesse and Hofmannsthal. It was chiefly for economic reasons—his family home passed of necessity into other hands and he felt responsible for his brothers—that he abandoned philology and began to study law (an older cousin was at this time professor of law at Uppsala University). In 1884, having passed his examination within a very short time, he received a scholarship enabling him to study at German universities, primarily those of Strasburg and Freiburg. He was a particular admirer of the legal historian von Amira, who lectured on old Nordic and Germanic jurisprudence. It was from this period of his life that Hammarskjöld became indissolubly bound to Germany; though it seems that in the Rhineland he adopted a somewhat ironic attitude towards Wilhelm's Germany, and never for a moment did he associate himself with that deformed offshoot of German chauvinism, National Socialism, which, to his grief, he lived long enough to experience.

While still very young he became a professor at Uppsala, though his exceptional administrative gifts resulted in his being frequently summoned to Stockholm on official duty; soon, indeed, he became Cabinet Minister. In 1905, after a period as president of the Göta high court of justice, he rejoined the government. In that year he was one of the Swedish negotiators at Karlstad, where the Union with Norway was so painfully dissolved. His was not a submissive temperament, yet he maintained an attitude of great moderation towards the Norwegian demands. If the Norwegians wanted to go, if they believed it to be politically advantageous to leave the Union, then of course no one should try to prevent them. (They were to pay the price for this when during the Second World War Hitler occupied their country, without their being able to put up any kind of effective resistance, while Sweden remained free.)

After a period as Swedish minister in Copenhagen, Hjalmar Hammarskjöld became lord-lieutenant of Uppsala, and in 1914 Prime Minister of Sweden, a post which he retained throughout most of the Great War. During that time he was the object of bitter hatred from socialists and liberals, and was even nicknamed "Hungerskjöld," being unjustly blamed for the national food-shortage. It is clear that he was autocratic, that he found difficulty in treating his government colleagues as equals and liked to make decisions without reference to them, confident in the infallibility of his insight and instinct. In 1917, after political storms which, for Sweden, were of unusual intensity and venom, he was forced to resign. An attempt was made, by presenting a huge list of sympathizers, to conceal the fact that he was then one of Sweden's most hated men.

Once again he became lord-lieutenant of Uppsala and enjoyed this unassuming and peaceful occupation. He appeared from time to time—always as an Independent—in the Riksdag, but was received as a rule with muted suspicion. In a speech concerning his great liberal opponent Karl Staaff, with whom he had successfully collaborated during the Union negotiations of 1905, he made this characteristic pronouncement:

"I fully appreciated the fact that when those tasks had been accomplished, our paths would diverge once more. Nevertheless I trusted that men who had once worked together selflessly to achieve a high aim could never be strangers to one another . . . This hope I still cherish. Common toil and strife, common hopes, common memories—be they bright or dark—will prove an enduring bond between us. All may be done, borne or accepted for love of our country, in our humble efforts to promote its welfare and protect it from misfortune and decline."

The following anecdote, related by his son as the conclusion to his Academy speech when succeeding to his father's chair, is characteristic of both men:

"When I look into the past in search of some situation that reflects the essence of Hjalmar Hammarskjöld, I pause at this recollection.

"It was late on the third day of the defence debate of 1925. Discussion in the upper house had been strongly colored by echoes of the great battles of 1914. Hjalmar Hammarskjöld, from his own—non-party—standpoint, had fought vigorously for his opinions, and had thereby become a personal target. It was in this situation that he spoke for the last time, ending with these words:

" 'Mention was made before the adjournment of a widely-held opinion that, in matters of defence, no worse adviser than myself could be found. Insofar as this may be true, I would ask all honorable members to forget—forget utterly —that I am pro-defence, so that the fact may present no obstacle to a favorable decision. *The identity of the person who takes the initiative or exerts influence is entirely immaterial to the great point at issue:* namely, *that our country's future may be secured!'*

"For the nineteen-year-old listener in the Strangers' Gallery of the Riksdag these words summarized a life based on faith in justice and in selfless service, under a responsibility that unites us all."

Hjalmar Hammarskjöld's most important legacy to his son was a belief in an international dispensation of justice. Of his father's life-long work to this end Dag Hammarskjöld writes:

"In trying to interpret the internationalism of which Hjalmar Hammarskjöld was the representative, I find the key in this: *Civitas Dei* was a dream from the past. The attempts of our own age to create an international organization with a common executive had not yet seen the light of day. Instead we glimpse here the idea of a world community where nation-states should live under the protection of an internationalism which derives its strength from the logical nature of justice itself, not from arbitrary decree, and consequently in which the only needful international organ is of a judicial nature."

Dag Hammarskjöld saw in his father a man of exceptionally forceful talents, which naturally carried him to the highest positions in the land.

Hjalmar Hammarskjöld's political achievements became in all essentials the object of misunderstanding and hatred. In an Uppsala poem written by Dag in 1959 while visiting the town of his childhood, the following cryptic lines occur:

> A box on the ear taught the boy
> That Father's name
> Was odious to them . . .

One may venture to guess at some incident in his schooldays: certain young contemporaries of his, from liberal-minded homes, may have been so strongly imbued with their fathers' disgust with the "Conservative, German-bought" Prime Minister Hammarskjöld as to attack his young son.

In itself the incident is unimportant. Yet throughout his life Dag Hammarskjöld brooded over his father's destiny: that man of duty who *could not* act otherwise than he did and who for that very reason was doomed to be hated. Would this be Dag's own fate? Could *no* unselfish, consistent life's work be carried through by the most gifted of men without his being exposed to enmity? His father belonged to a form of Old Lutheran Christianity whose center of gravity was the fulfilment of duty. From his image and destiny the thoughts of the son turned to Christ, who in greater measure and without guilt was slain for his love and steadfastness.

We shall see how this theme became central to Dag Hammarskjöld's own life.

Towards his end Hjalmar Hammarskjöld lived quietly and perhaps not without bitterness in his Stockholm flat. His son delineates him in the opening of his Academy speech:

"It was in October of last year. Anacreon lay on the writing-table. The empty chair was turned towards Humlegården, where flocks of jackdaws were settling for the night in the tops of the autumn-red trees round the Royal Library— those jackdaws whose apparently senseless battles he had witnessed with ironic amusement during his last years, seeing in them the typification of the heathen raging violently together and the people imagining a vain thing; these flocks which during his long solitude had become ever more longed for, and greeted as messengers from the plain and the towers of the Uppsala of his youth and manhood."

And he writes, in words that were to be as applicable to him as to his father:

"A mature man is his own judge. When all is said and done, his one firm support is his loyalty to his own convictions. The counsel of others may be welcome and valuable, but it does not release him from responsibility; therefore he may become very lonely. Therefore, too, he must deliberately risk being accused of stiff-necked self-sufficiency. As the war went on and difficulties increased, this was the fate of Hjalmar Hammarskjöld."

Around 1930 the writer of this book saw a great deal of Dag Hammarskjöld's mother, of whom I shall soon speak, and visited the Hammarskjölds' house in Stockholm. On such occasions I received a daunting impression of the father's reserve and isolation, and perhaps also of his bitterness and disillusionment: he could be glimpsed as a massive Småland block of granite, away there in his study, barely aware of the young guests in his house. At once the question arose: was the isolation of this important man attributable only to the fact that he had done his duty—done what he thought right? Was he not perhaps also paying the price of his self-assurance, his insensibility towards others, his want of love for ordinary fellow-beings? Political memoirs present an alarming picture of the great

man's self-esteem, contempt for humanity and
lack of psychological sensitivity.

Finally, we must stress once more Hjalmar
Hammarskjöld's life-long interest in setting up an
international system of justice. He was very often employed in foreign affairs, above all as the
Swedish delegate to other peace-conferences at
The Hague, and later as arbitrator in various international disputes, including that of Casa-
blanca.

Opinions may vary as to the manner in which,
as Prime Minister of Sweden, Hjalmar Hammarskjöld expressed in action his principles of
justice. His son gives this account:

"When Hjalmar Hammarskjöld so persistently
and sharply emphasized the principles of popular
justice—both as established by treaty and as he
considered they should be extended and developed in any new and unforeseen situation—his
motives were quite certainly ideological, at least
in part. In a joint Scandinavian note sent to the
combatants in the autumn of 1914 we find the
familiar words: the combatants should after the
war be content to find inviolate some of the basic
principles which they formerly valued. The
political weight of the argument here presented
may be confirmed by anyone who has had the
opportunity of testing it. Yet the phrase is more
than an argument. It reflects the conviction of a
man who desired justice—desired it in the knowl-

edge of how thin the wall is between culture and barbarism—thus anticipating the bitter experience of later decades.

"While Hjalmar Hammarskjöld unhesitatingly committed himself to the concept of justice, he was well aware how vague and imperfect were the rules which reflected this concept in international circles. It was certainly foreign to his ideas that a small country like Sweden should attempt to rescue them [the combatant nations] and ferry them into the years of peace at the expense of its own vital interests; the time might come when compromise was as natural for a neutral state as for a warring one, but until such a situation arose neutral peoples had especial obligations to the future.

"Other than ideological views of popular justice had to be taken into consideration. 'What the critics didn't see,' he once said, 'is that for a small country popular justice is the only remaining argument, and that therefore, in its own interest the defence of justice is worthy of sacrifice.' "

Dag Hammarskjöld's father was a man of ideas, a great but detested politician, with considerable resources and brilliant gifts, but with only meager capacity for making direct and warm contact with his fellow-men. He was remote even from his youngest son. His reported remark: "If I'd had Dag's brains I should have gone far" is of course apocryphal. More convincing is another anecdote. On studying Dag's brilliant graduation report—the young man naturally took a First—his only comment is said to have been: "Ake's was better."

I may add that when Dag gave me the manuscript of his Academy speech he said in a quiet, diffident voice:

"Well, you know me—you'll realize that I never knew my father as well as this during his lifetime . . ."

Chapter 2

DAG HAMMARSKJÖLD's mother exerted a very different influence on her son. He gave this description of her in his Academy speech:

"In 1890 he founded his home. In his wife he found a resolute loyalty to personal ideals similar to his own; in many other respects Agnes Almquist was different. Her chief traits, which seem to me characteristic of her family, had once appeared with particular vividness and with the disturbing overtones of genius in her father's half-brother, the author of *Amorina:* that is to say, a radically democratic and, if one will, an 'evangelical' view of mankind; a child's open attitude to life; an anti-rationalism with strong emotional undercurrents. With these qualities and the generous giving out of herself to those near to her and to strangers, to which such qualities impelled her, she brought into Hjalmar Hammarskjöld's life elements which count for a great deal in the interpretation of his later development."

The author of *Amorina* was the romantic poet
Carl Jonas Love Almquist who, after what was
in many respects a splendid literary career, attempted murder in connection with forgery and
was compelled to flee to America, where he led a
most wretched existence. He is the great example
in Swedish literature of poetic genius combined
with moral dissolution.

Agnes Hammarskjöld was her husband's opposite in almost every respect. She was warm and
gushing; it was hard to tell at times whether she
was laughing or crying; she had so overflowing
and generous a heart that no one who came near
her could avoid her eager—sometimes perhaps
slightly ill-considered but always warm—solici-
tude. I speak here of my own experience. When
I married, this grand and singular lady wired
warm good wishes "from your motherly old bat-
tleaxe Agnes Hammarskjöld." In 1926, when I
had my one and only dispute with Dag Hammarskjöld, she at once attempted with copious tears
to bring about our reconciliation, in which she
easily succeeded. She was so close a friend of
Nathan Söderblom, the theologian Archbishop
of Uppsala, that—being born on the same day—
they were known as "the twins." She was a dog-
matically vague but emotional and strongly
committed Lutheran Christian. Dag's atheist companions later recalled with an ironical smile how
out of courtesy he accompanied her to church on

Sundays: so brilliantly gifted a man could of course have no Christian faith . . . It is also told how he once arrived a quarter of an hour late for a rendezvous with a young lady, and gave as a fully adequate explanation and apology that it would have been quite impossible to interrupt a conversation with his (certainly very garrulous) mother.

The hostess in the mighty Uppsala castle, where the lord-lieutenant has his official apartments, was an engaging and original lady who perhaps even more than her husband set her stamp upon Dag. I would like at this stage to quote what in maturity he wrote about his Christian faith:

"Faith is a state of the mind and the soul. In this sense we can understand the words of the Spanish mystic St. John of the Cross: 'Faith is the union of God with the soul.' The language of religion is a set of formulas which register a basic spiritual experience. It must not be regarded as describing, in terms to be defined by philosophy, the reality which is accessible to our senses and which we can analyse with the tools of logic. I was late in understanding what this meant. When I finally reached that point, the beliefs in which I was once brought up and which, in fact, had given my life direction even while my intellect still challenged their validity, were recognized by me as mine in their own right, and by my free choice. I feel that I can endorse those convictions without any compromise with the demands of that intellectual honesty which is the very key to maturity of mind."

Such is his plain statement: the faith in which his mother brought him up he was in time to recognize as his own.

It is evident that Agnes Hammarskjöld bore a very special love for her brilliant youngest son. In her somewhat unthinking way she would explain how, after the birth of her three elder boys, she had yearned for a daughter, and for a long time had let little Dag (born when she was in her forties) wear girl's clothes. Dag was a markedly virile person, entirely free from feminine traits of character; yet he had no difficulty in accepting his mother's kindly despotism and volubility: I can still see his indulgent smile when at a tea-party given for me and my fiancée, at which he served us, she began rather indiscreetly describing her life and her family's, and her sullen husband. Dag lived with his parents until well on into manhood; even as a high-ranking official he dutifully observed the domestic time-table. One may, without wishing to touch upon a delicate theme, guess at some connection between, on the one hand, Dag's attitude to his devotedly loved, exacting mother and his stern, reserved demigod of a father, and, on the other, the fact that throughout his life he remained not only unmarried but so far as is known without any realistic contact with the opposite sex. The one woman for whom he felt tenderness and attachment he immediately renounced on discovering that one of his friends was also paying court to her. Afterwards he became one of that family's loyal friends; the renunciation seems to have been made without the slightest effort, though it could be observed that whenever he met the couple he always stubbornly addressed his remarks to the husband, never to the wife.

In his youth Dag's brother Sten wrote a novel: *The Boy Who Bowed to God*. In it he gives a description of his mother:

"When she was to leave him, were it for only a few hours, he felt the emptiness gnawing at him. And if she had to be away for half a day or more, he would always stand outside the garden gate when she went, his heart aching with grief. He felt as if he would never see her again. The hour before she left for a party, or the like, he took care to spend with her while she changed, following her everywhere about the room. The loss of her cast its shadow before."

Sten Söderberg, one of Dag's finest portrayers, makes this comment:

"The difference was that Dag was more often able to be with his mother than Sten, who was sometimes confined to bed. Dag was his mother's gentleman-in-waiting, her page, her faithful and considerate attendant."

The following extract is taken from the same writer's authoritative account:

"It was the castle of Uppsala that was to be

Dag Hammarskjöld's true childhood home. In this the lord-lieutenant occupied a suite of rooms that might most nearly be compared with one of the larger, gloomier flats in the Östermalm district of Stockholm. The rebuilding of the castle was not undertaken until the depression of the thirties, as an emergency work-program for the unemployed. But the gloom of those rooms was never noticeable so long as Agnes Hammarskjöld was there to dispel it with her vivacity and warmth."

The whole of that ancient castle of the Vasas was a story-book world. What is now the hall of state was then a wonderful playroom; mysterious passages ran between the massive walls; in the towers were circular banquet-rooms (including the court of session of the provincial government, which was at the disposal of the lord-lieutenant when entertaining) and, elsewhere, dark dungeons that whispered ghostly tales: the grim reverse-side of traditional glories. Here it was that Dag led his young friends on thrilling explorations, and even when he had reached the age of his first dances he could lure a few friends from the ballroom and buffet into the winding passages of the fortress.

Although the residence of a provincial governor must always be something of a public place, Agnes Hammarskjöld contrived to preserve its homelike character, and to imbue it with an atmosphere of solid respectability: a shield against the irritations and clashes of the outside world in which Hjalmar Hammarskjöld was so deeply involved.

Nevertheless it is clear that Dag's father often brought the problems of the day to the dinner-table. He reported what was going on as Europe approached a world war, as the kingdom was split into two seething camps over the question of defence, and as hope brightened again and sprang up round the League of Nations. And he discussed these questions with his sons: gravely perhaps with the elder ones, if more playfully with the others. Yet it is said that even little Dag had views of his own.

His mother's anchorage in the gospels must have meant a great deal to the family. Hjalmar Hammarskjöld's beliefs were presumably of a more conventional order: his Bible and hymn-book were well-worn; he was president of the Bible Society and, impelled by his conservative nature, he "stood guard"—as is still so often said in election-speeches—"over Christian values." This does not necessarily imply any very deep involvement. But in the mother's case it was beyond doubt; and every Sunday Dag accompanied her to church, which Hjalmar Hammarskjöld seldom found time to attend. Here I must quote what Jon Olof Söderblom, a childhood friend of Dag's, has told me:

"Some time in the thirties I was to be god-
father to a friend's child, and unlike most other
members of the christening party I went first to
hear the sermon in Engelbrekt's Church. Not far
from me I noticed Dag. This was nothing
unusual: childhood customs were ingrained in
him, as in me."

It is the duty of a governor's lady to be active
in good works. Before the social revolution and
the formation of the welfare state to which both
Bo and Dag were to contribute so much, such
activity often took the form of a benevolent, society hobby, to be engaged in for pleasure and
for the benefit of one's conscience. For Agnes
Hammarskjöld this Lady Bountiful attitude was
probably not enough. She had the faculty of put-
ting herself in another's place and knew that the
aim must be to set people on their feet, and not
just feed them. There are instances of her drawing other leading figures with her into this, and
her son Dag accompanied her on her visits to
people in distress.

There are also idylls from the days of childhood when the father of the family shared in the
fun. Sten tells:

"When on some snow-laden, sharp December
morning after the end of term I was allowed to
go with my father and choose a Christmas tree
. . . I knew that many glorious days lay ahead,
beginning with Christmas Eve when he cut the

gigantic round cheese that the Dairy Farm Association always presented to their president, and we later gathered in the dining-room round the long table which was laid in the old-fashioned manner. My father insisted that all feast days should be celebrated in the way he had been accustomed to since childhood; therefore Småland province was always a holiday guest in our Uppland home.

"This was especially true on Christmas Eve when family and servants gathered round the huge tree and my mother read the Gospel. Easter customs, with verses on the eggs before they were boiled, were observed too, as surely as the midsummer expedition in an open landau to some alluring place where the scent and color of the flowers brought us the rich essence of the Swedish summer."

Chapter 3

As AN undergraduate at Uppsala Hammarskjöld
read history of literature, philosophy, French
and economics. He was nineteen when he took
his first examination and the degree of Phil.
Cand. He once complained to the wife of Archbishop Söderblom:

"I thought I should be reading about the
progress of ideas through the ages, not wasting
attention on the love-affairs of authors . . ."

The wise lady noticed his interest in philosophy, and asked:

"Haven't you started on Pascal yet?"

In his youth he had thought of reading theol-
ogy. He used to talk a great deal about his father's friend Archbishop Söderblom, and I remember his giving this man my own first book,
which among other things dealt with Söderblom's "Christian mysticism," comparing it with
the Swedish writers Erik Blomberg and Pär
Lagerkvist (whom Söderblom firmly rejected).

Even when he was about to leave Sweden to take over his high post in New York, Hammarskjöld found time to pay a last visit to the Archbishop's wife, with whom he was on close terms.

While a student he lived at home in the castle, but mixed normally with his contemporaries, of whom a number have become leading figures.

For his doctor's degree Dag Hammarskjöld chose to take economics; but at this point there occurred something that astonished him—and others. He had an unusual professor—to put it no more strongly—who refused to accept Hammarskjöld's thesis. On two different occasions he acidly rejected the young student's notes for this paper; the first time alleging that most of it was wrong, and the second time with the words: "What's the good of this? It's no more than what I've said already . . ." Hammarskjöld was upset, but as the tutor was a professor of law and he himself had thought of a career in government he quickly studied for the degree of Juris Cand. (Bachelor of Law).

Even at this time Hammarskjöld was very much alone. He was living in the Uppsala of the twenties, that is to say, he was surrounded by companions who for the most part were spiritually and religiously unawakened, and to whom he had to speak in another language—a language foreign to his soul. He played the dangerous role of model boy and student; he gathered *laudaturs* as others pick plums, he concealed his superiority and was careful not to give himself airs; he was friendly, positive and a good, if somewhat abstracted, listener.

My wife, who belonged to a French club in Uppsala which he also joined, describes how he stood out from the other students, who in comparison with him appeared shallow and lacking in seriousness; to a person of any observation it was clear that he carried an inner world within him, to whose echoes he listened eagerly, but about which he seldom found opportunity to speak.

I met Dag Hammarskjöld at the Sigtuna Foundation in 1930. He was walking up and down the arcades with a lawbook in his hand. He studied systematically, calmly and without panic; therefore very effectively. I noted with amazement in my diary that Dag was the most remarkable student I had ever met in Sweden; he was *ratio pura*, I wrote naively, and I predicted that he would become prime minister.

Just at this time I had discovered in France and Germany new masters who dimmed the lustre of my former Swedish idols. In various essays, later collected in the book *Den kristna falangen* (The Christian Falange, 1934), I attempted to write something about these spiritual experiences, of which I found no equivalent in our country, and felt as if I were talking in a vacuum, without resonance. (Ten years later the climate had changed.)

The first person I met who was not only open and receptive to the religious battle among the young élite of France but had good knowledge of the whole *renouveau catholique* was Hammarskjöld. I had no idea of this. In 1930, while I was working on my first novel in Sigtuna, he paced the arcades and calmly, methodically studied for his Juris. Cand. I pitied him his drab destiny, but found that he was in no way oppressed or burdened by all that dead material; his soul lived on beside it, lively and untrammeled. We discussed together some of the chapters in my novel; he was my first reader, and I listened in wonder to his remarks. He was unassuming: a model of tact and delicacy. He understood everything. In the course of many walks together we planned a defence of Christianity, a sort of apologia against the so-called Hagerström school of philosophy, which he had studied and thought out but did not fear.

I noted in my diary that I had met an exceptional young man, a character of unusual integrity and brilliant understanding, as well as chivalrous, courteous and serious. Never before in Sweden had I encountered a young man of these qualities. None of my Stockholm friends took any interest in the things that preoccupied me; I couldn't even discuss them with anyone of my own age and had to cultivate such interests on my own. Dag was the first Swede who shared them.

Not only this, he took them in deadly earnest, reading and meditating upon what were for me sacred texts. At this time—1930—he had not yet studied the mystics, St. John of the Cross, St. Theresa of Avila and Thomas à Kempis, who were later to be of decisive significance in his spiritual development, but he was familiar with Pascal, and one had only to mention some saint hitherto unknown to him for him to gather relevant material for study.

When in 1934 I published *The Christian Falange* he wrote to me:

"You have interpreted voices and lives which only a few of our generation in this country have known, and which none of us others have had the ability or strength to make accessible to all those whom in these days they must chiefly concern."

The phrasing shows that he himself had dreamt or considered the possibility of writing about these things. In letters written during his last years in New York he implied that he had not abandoned the plan; he was preparing a book in which he would speak openly of his spiritual experiences.

"I hope I shall have enough patience, humility and serenity left when I'm able to return to a life along these lines. Then perhaps I shall be able to say in the right way some part of what ought to be said."

In 1932 he wrote to me:

"I am much interested in your essays on Rivière and others. To me, as you may remember, Rivière is one of the great ones."

Jacques Rivière was the French critic, practically unknown in Sweden, who during his German imprisonment in the First World War had written a diary which appeared under the title *A la Trace de Dieu.* I had been shaken by it, and mentioned its author in an essay. Dag already knew of him. I was staggered. A remarkable lawyer and economist, I thought. Other divinities of mine he knew only slightly, but he began to read them: Claudel, Bloy, Péguy. When I asked him cautiously whether he was familiar with the Swedish mystic Bertil Ekman who lost his life in the mountains, he answered that he was and that Ekman had meant a great deal to him.

I asked, because at this time Bertil Ekman was very much in my mind. His only book is *Scattered Pages from the Posthumous Papers of Bertil Ekman* (Strödda blad ur Bertil Ekmans efterlämnade papper, 1923). He was a young Uppsala student who died at the age of 26, during a tour in the mountains with his friend and inspirer Harald Alm, a wellknown teacher at Siljan School. It has been pointed out that as late as 1955 Hammarskjöld wrote in Ekman's style in a letter, when expressing his delight at the release of the American airmen who had been im-

prisoned in China: "Today we accomplished
something, God and I. That is to say it was God
who built while I stood below with the paint-
pot, shouting." In Ekman, Hammarskjöld encountered thoughts that were never to loosen
their hold on his mind. Ekman once wrote:

"It is not enough to believe in immortality
with mind and heart alone; that belief must become a part of the *will*, which may then be
wholly directed towards death. It is not death
that will come to Everyman, but Everyman who
will advance upon death . . ."

And another time:

"Death must inspire longing *towards* life, not
away from it. When shall the vigor of death
send us lithe and light-footed on our ways about
the earth? Whereas life weighs down, death is
light as air. Whereas life divides, death unites."

The poet Erik Lindegren, Hammarskjöld's
successor in the Swedish Academy, reminds us
that this closely resembles what Hammarskjöld
wrote during his New York period:

"Not to encumber the earth—No histrionic
Excelsior, but just this: not to encumber the
earth."

One day in 1931 my wife and I were talking
with Hammarskjöld about Bertil Ekman. Dag
quoted from memory the whole or part of this
poem, so it must have made an especially strong
impression on him:

I see the bold seafarers of God
Their sun-burned wills, their brows serene.
Smoothly glide their sails upon the river,
Slowly, more slowly, in a single line.

I see them take each other's hands:
A chain of brothers.
The sails are gilded by the glow of evening.
Proud and bleeding the sun goes down.
Now has struck the hour of mankind's evening.
The sails glide out
Into the vast, rejoicing sea of God
With its eternal deeps
Its limitless expanse . . .

Bertil Ekman's closest friend Harald Alm—
who went with him on his last tour in the mountains, and found his body—wrote in a fine article
on Ekman that appeared in *Perspektiv* 1964,
1:
"Has not Dag Hammarskjöld's *life* shown a
peculiar kinship with Bertil's *vision* of death
and life?"
A note from *Markings* shows that Dag's first
human ideal came near to Ekman's image of sun-
browned wills and pure brows:
"The aura of victory that surrounds a man of
good will, the sweetness of soul which emanates
from him—a flavor of cranberries and cloud-
berries, a touch of frost and fiery skies."

At that time, in the early thirties, Dag Hammarskjöld kept this spiritual world of his concealed in all essentials. There were reasons for this. I have mentioned the Hagerström philosophy that dominated Uppsala. Dag was his friends' friend and was careful to abstain from unnecessary criticism; yet throughout his time in Sweden he could speak very acidly about the torment of talking "baby-talk" with his companions. When he tried to touch on deeper themes, on religious and metaphysical aspects of life, they completely failed to understand him. It was sometimes uncomfortable to observe how people to whom he had never even hinted at his inner world fondly believed themselves his intimates. Perhaps in this respect he was a little too skilful; if he had a use for people he let them imagine that they were his bosom friends. They never knew him.

To escape his wooden-headed Uppsala professor Dag moved to what was then *Stockholms Högskola* or college, where in 1933 he took part in debates. When I wrote congratulating him on his duel with the young Olympian Gunnar Myrdal, his first opponent—an encounter which had much impressed me—he replied somberly:

"Thank you for your great kindness in attending the debate, and for your letter which gave me deep and sincere pleasure. You would have heard from me earlier, if the committee-business [i.e., the enquiry into unemployment] hadn't continued—with increasing urgency—immedi- ately after the disputation, when I was pretty tired and therefore worked slowly. The result was that my personal interests went by the board.

"I don't share your opinion of the debate; from an intellectual point of view it was just a circus, with a dialectical tight-rope act as the main item. The ritual seemed to me morally inferior. Yet in an odd way it was a continuation of the duel between two different styles, which I tried to introduce through the stubborn presentation of the theme.

"I disagree with you even more strongly about the intellectual level of us economists. What may support your impression is the extroversion, the ease in public, which results from training in political discussion and adminstration and which gives economists the air of intellectual strength. I believe that as *scholars* the students of science are, generally speaking, of better material, though they lack the surface polish that would enable them to do themselves justice. But this view arises from my hostility to certain features of economics, and I am therefore rather suspicious of it."

Hammarskjöld's doctoral thesis dealt with the levelling out of booms and slumps. His friend and opponent Gunnar Myrdal, later to be world-famous as an economist, has said that the thesis was written as it were "with the left hand": that is, without real inclination or commitment. He says too that Hammarskjöld "was aware that he was unfitted for a career of research. Great research, like great art, demands not only intelligence and health, which Dag Hammarskjöld possessed in abundance, but also a freedom from inhibitions—even to the point of recklessness—which he never had. In his relation to scholarship, as to literature and art, he deliberately confined himself to the role of exquisite connoisseur."

I do not believe that this is altogether accurate. Dag Hammarskjöld considered, with some bitterness, that no one had properly understood his thesis. Professor Gösta Bagge, whose subject it was, seems to have been unable to grasp the subtly abstract trains of thought, and marked the work *cum laude;* that is, the average mark given to all reasonably good theses which nevertheless have not carried the study of the theme noticeably further. Myrdal himself would have given him only slightly higher marks, which brought about a certain rift between him and Hammarskjöld. Hammarskjöld was quite simply hurt not to have been given in this case, as in all others, the highest award *laudatur*, "the only one that would have satisfied the demands he made upon himself"

(Myrdal). Myrdal's opinion was that "his handling of ideas was inhibited when he went beyond a particular and technically practical problem. His otherwise orderly forms of thought and speech became involved, obscure and confused." My own belief, based on what Hammarskjöld himself said, is that he would most likely have continued in economic science but for this blow to his pride. Privately I thought that the experience might turn out to be quite good for the young genius.

In the same memorial article Gunnar Myrdal writes that "his contacts with people were intellectual and disciplined, not instinctive and natural . . . Those who knew Dag Hammarskjöld do not think of him as an unfeeling, coldly calculating person. On the contrary, his personality was explosively emotional, though the emotions were under control."

This tallies exactly with my first impressions of him, such as I noted in my diary. In his youth Hammarskjöld was very reserved, even shy. Both of us, as young men, had shivered separately in the same sort of isolation, and therefore made rapid contact. But the contact had its difficulties. He was distressed by his inability to establish direct, warm relationships, and at the beginning of 1931 he wrote:

"My bad habit of reducing all conversations to 'essentials,' intellectual and moral cubism, if you like, leads to a dry-as-dust sincerity which only in rare contexts can be of interest to others, and which in any case pre-supposes in them a corresponding need to make the fullest use of every instant—in faith. In this way I have been led to overestimate companionship *à deux* compared with sociability on a larger scale."

(I never understood what he meant by the words "in faith" in this letter.)

This theme recurs again and again even in his later diaries. In 1950 he writes:

"Only tell people what is of importance to them. Only ask them what you need to know. In both cases, that is, limit the conversation to what the speaker really possesses—argue only in order to reach a conclusion. Think aloud only with those to whom this means something. Don't let small talk fill up the time and the silence except as a medium for bearing unexpressed messages between two people who are attuned to each other. A dietary for those who have learned by experience the truth of the saying, 'For every idle word . . .' But hardly popular in social life."

In the same year he notes:

"When the evening of being together was over, a feeling of emptiness bordering on guilt brought on the anguish which inevitably accompanies sloth and inadequacy.

"The evening had not only been meaningless; it had been unnecessary. Staged for reasons which,

in a human relation of such an ordinary character, were a surrender to the mortal sin of sloth.
The comedy had to be played out to the end,
filled up, as, in the circumstances, was only to be
expected, with an idle chatter which degraded the
living reality."

This, as self-discipline, is impressive; but it is
also somewhat disturbing. Dag Hammarskjöld
approved only of deliberate conversation which
aimed at "results"! He knew little of carefree
playing with words, and how without thought of
making an effect one can use the magic of words
to create an atmosphere of warmth which may
mean something much more in a fellow-being's
life than an intellectual "result." The word-
games of poetry and paradox played with
women and children—of those he knew almost
nothing.

Yet he longed for this world, from which he
was shut out.

In 1950 he wrote in his diary:

"How undisguised your thick-skinned self-
satisfied loneliness appeared before his naked
agony as he struggled to make a living contact.
How difficult you found it to help, when confronted in another by your own problem—
uncorrupted."

*　　*　　*

"Suddenly I saw he was more real to himself
than I am to myself, and that what was required

of me was to experience this reality of his not as an object but as a subject—and *more* real than mine."

One can see from this that he had read Martin Buber, and perhaps Gabriel Marcel. As early as 1930 I discussed Buber with Dag Hammarskjöld, who later revered Buber as a great authority. He had begun a translation of Buber's work *I and Thou* but never finished it. He told his publisher that he wanted the book to appear in Swedish because it expressed almost exactly his own views.

Martin Buber's doctrine may perhaps be summarized in this sentence: "I-thou can only be uttered with the whole of our being; I-it can never be uttered with the whole of our being." We find the same distinctions in the writings of the Frenchman Gabriel Marcel and—much earlier—in those of E. G. Geijer, the Swede. A special feature of Martin Buber, and one that impressed Hammarskjöld, was his view of the ingrained habit in modern man of always suspecting the person he is conversing with of dishonesty. Hammarskjöld quoted Buber in June 1950 at a lunch at Cambridge University, in an address on "Man's Greatest Challenge": *

* Extract from *Dag Hammarskjöld: Servant of Peace:* A Selection edited by Wilder Foote. Harper & Row, 1963.

"There have always been countless situations in which a man believes his life-interest demands that he suspect the other of making it his object to appear otherwise than he is . . . In our time something basically different has been added . . . One no longer merely fears that the other will voluntarily dissemble, but one takes it for granted that he cannot do otherwise . . . The other communicates to me the perspective that he has acquired on a certain subject, but I do not really take cognizance of his communication as knowledge. I do not take it seriously as a contribution to the information about this subject, but rather I listen for what drives the other to say what he says, for an unconscious motive . . . Since it is the idea of the other, it is for me an 'ideology.' My main task in my intercourse with my fellow-man becomes more and more . . . to see through and unmask him . . . With this changed basic attitude . . . the mistrust between man and man has become existential. This is so indeed in a double sense: It is first of all no longer the uprightness, the honesty of the other which is in question, but the inner integrity of his existence itself . . . Nietzsche knew what he was doing when he praised 'the art of mistrust,' and yet he did not know. For this game naturally only becomes complete as it becomes reciprocal . . . Hence one may foresee in the future a degree of reciprocity in existential mistrust where speech will turn into dumbness and sense into madness."

When in 1931 I got engaged, he wrote:

"It has always struck me as grotesque that when we perform some action that stands out as central to our life, we should be exposed to well-meaning salvoes of good wishes for our happiness, from the bystanders. What do they know as a rule of the 'happiness' that is bound up with our action?

"I know you too well even to feel tempted to bring out such phrases—sullied, too, like masks concealing inner indifference—yet I do not know you well enough for any letter of mine 'in nakedness of spirit' to be anything but an intrusion into a sanctuary closed to me. My good wishes are therefore a prayer that behind inadequate phrases you may feel what Rivière would have called *'une profonde sympathie avec l'évènement'*—with all that this meant to him in general applied here to you and yours.

"How frightful our poverty is when we try to give others something of ourselves—something that may mean a little to them: that solidarity which has been dressed up in such high-flown paraphrases as sympathy and friendship, though it would be better expressed by 'will' and 'comradeship.' Even in a non-egocentric sense there is an incurable loneliness of the soul—an inability to live in such a way that others may know what they can count upon in us. Only this morning you gave me a hard-handed reminder of this! Don't think me presumptuous! Perhaps even in writing these lines I go too far, since we have met so seldom. Yet why should the rarity of meetings prevent one from acknowledging solidarity in the deepest sense?

"As usual in such situations the root of the matter is very simple but also very real: something that is our own in its human poverty, behind all the thousand affectations of social life— all its viewpoints and the interplay of supposed interests. That this must seem to you a trifle compared with what you possess in others, or are confronted by, I know more than well. If it has any value to you I am glad. To me the ineradicable shyness of this morning is a curse, and the conventional, awkward conversation a lie.

"You should go into a hospital if one's to imagine that one isn't taking up your time by a visit!"

I was more primitive than Dag and was unaware of having given him a "hard-handed reminder" of the distance between us. But I had noticed something else.

In Dag, whom I admired and liked more than anyone else of my generation, there was so vast and unsatisfied a need of tenderness that he not seldom appeared to be in real distress. He was masculine all through; there was nothing effeminate in his nature. He was not afraid of women, and could speak expertly on feminine beauty; yet I sometimes felt that for all his polite talk at parties he never visually discriminated between a shapely woman and, say, a sofa or a chair. In later years he created a harmonious atmosphere for himself, and was surrounded by highly gifted men to whose wives he displayed courteous attention. He had found his own, virile way of life: that of the man of action, the political leader, the aesthetic sybarite. In his youth he lacked this Olympian assurance. When he approached me with a look that begged timidly for understanding, agreement, warmth—without his being able to find the corresponding, liberating tone of voice—I was worried. I couldn't give him what he sought; my notion of friendship was coarser than his, and when he invited me to what in his peculiar phrase he termed friendship "in faith," I drew back, slightly scared.

But one thing is certain: his demeanor and his letters had a powerful, impressive and often crushing impact on me. From the beginning I felt very strongly that this young man was purer than perhaps anyone I had ever met.

Dag Hammarskjöld impressed me greatly with his maturity—Christian maturity. I wrote in my diary: "Dag is a man, *nada menos que todo un hombre*," nothing less than a whole man. Never before had I met such a companion. Later, when in essays and novels I wrote of personal Christian conflict, his figure was often before my mind's eye, though I never attempted a portrait.

These personal impressions of mine are confirmed by extracts from Hammarskjöld's posthumously-published diary. In this book he gives youthful expression to his longing for purity, heroism, clarity, integrity. An early poem runs:

Smiling, sincere, incorruptible—
His body disciplined and limber.
A man who had become what he could,
And was what he was—
Ready at any moment to gather everything
Into one simple sacrifice.

Tomorrow we shall meet,
Death and I—
And he shall thrust his sword
Into one who is wide awake.

But in the meantime how grievous the memory
Of hours frittered away.

Here is all his young idealism. Notice that the idea of sacrifice, which later was to be the center of his thinking, was already present in the mind of the twenty-year-old!

He notes in an aphorism the necessity of being oneself. His aim is "—to become a mirror in which, according to the degree of purity of heart you have attained, the greatness of life will be reflected."

He was still unacquainted with the Christian way of life. "Never accept what can be gained by giving in," he says. "Life yields only to the conqueror . . ." he was later to alter his opinion; he understood perfectly what Simone Weil meant by her expression "waiting."

Quite early in life he became aware of his loneliness. "Every deed and every relationship is surrounded by an atmosphere of silence," he says rather cryptically, and goes on: "Friendship needs no words—it is solitude delivered from the anguish of loneliness." Thus even friendship is regarded as a solitude.

In a memorial poem written in 1959 he gives a fascinating picture of the university town of his youth:

FROM UPPSALA

Red evenings in March. News of death.
Begin anew—
What has ended?

Night. Plains. An empty hall.
In the window niche
She waits for the sunrise.

Cockchafers. Sorb-apple blossom.
Lilacs conversing
After bedtime.

The trees pant. Silence.
An irresolute raindrop furrows
The dark pane.

A cone of light in the fog.
A winter moth dancing
Round the lamp post.

Grey snow-walls. Warm horse-dung.
The houses stretch themselves.
Stale in the morning.

Some days later he continues this eerie and al-
lusive poem of his youth. He sees

A church spire, erect on the plain
Like a phallus.

He remembers the sexual awakening of his
boyhood:

The boy in the forest
Throws off his best Sunday suit
And plays naked.
* * *

**Dag
Hammarskjöld**

Black shooting-stars,
The swallows utter shrill cries
As they mate in mid-air.

*   *   *

He lowered his eyes
Lest he should see the body
To lust after it.

*   *   *

Denied the Sought-After
He longed to deserve
To be the Sought-After.

*   *   *

Honeysuckle.
In a grey twilight
His sensuality awoke.

These little poems need no commentary. They portray the common human experience of the sweetness of desire and its first fears, of youthful timidity and dread. When he meets young, enticing, feminine beauty, he lowers his eyes. And he entertains a dangerous thought: being denied the one he wanted, he must himself be the sought-after.

Chapter 4

AFTER HIS doctorate Dag Hammerskjöld quickly made a career for himself in government service. As secretary of the committee set up to enquire into unemployment he had the opportunity of calling in a number of his young fellow-economists, and it can be said that, if not the creator, he was at least the organiser of the "Stockholm School" of economics. He was the first of the young economists to use the term "planned economy" as a guide-line for future Swedish policy, says Gunnar Myrdal, who afterwards played the very role of radical economic researcher that Hammarskjöld dropped after his doctorate. Hammarskjöld was soon associated with the National Bank of Sweden—the oldest note-issuing bank in existence in the world—and in time became chairman of the board. His next step was his appointment as permanent secretary to the Finance Department. For ten years he worked

with Ernst Wigforss, the eminent Social-Democrat politician, who frankly acknowledges that
the moderate form of planned economy adopted
so successfully by Sweden was as much the work
of Hammarskjöld as of himself. Wigforss later
expressed surprise that Hammarskjöld was attracted neither to science nor to politics. He did
realize, however, that Hammarskjöld would
never fit into any of the Swedish political parties.
Wigforss says that he regarded him as a "tory-
democrat, a highly modernized tory-democrat,"
and goes on:

"His emotional attitude towards people and
class-differences seemed to me to be not far re-
moved from my own, and he appeared to consider that a democratic levelling-out policy was
one to be pursued as a matter of course. His view
of the public's role was tinged with an older conservatism, which regarded the state as a highly-
developed form of human society and the guard-
ian of universal values as opposed to private interests. A liberal suspicion of the state, which
soon set its stamp on political conservatism, was
hardly compatible with Hammarskjöld's attitude
to the state's function in economic life; an attitude which placed him more decisively among
the 'planned' economists than among the economic liberals. But the difference in both tradi-
tion and age-group also formed a barrier against
the kind of socialism that existed among Social

Democrats. How much the family traditions in government service counted with him I will not venture to guess. But he belonged to a younger generation with a greater fear of splendid abstractions, in relation to social and other human problems, than he believed was felt by the social-democrat Minister of Finance."

Thus spoke Ernst Wigforss, Hammarskjöld's social-democrat chief and close friend.

Hammarskjöld's career continued: he became permanent Secretary of State in the Swedish Foreign Office and later a member of the Government. He could hardly attain a higher position in his own country.

His colleagues have given many descriptions of him at this time, and they mention among other things his phenomenal capacity for work. To this day his working hours at the Ministry are legendary. As a rule he came back to his office after dinner and seldom went home until the small hours. When under great pressure he would suddenly disappear into the Jämtland mountains. Though not in the virtuoso class of skiers, he was an enthusiast, and would return after a week or so, sunburned and fit. I must admit, however, that I have never understood all the talk about his tremendous efficiency: it must have originated with people who were frustrated or inhibited in their own work. A man who found it necessary to resort to the night-hours to accomplish his life's task is not the ideal leader of a complex team. He was not at all quick; in writing especially he had great stylistic difficulty. Yet he often displayed greater resources than his colleagues, merely because he was free to concentrate all his energy on his work. He once said to me (it may have been a quotation): "I have the impression that most married men devote 90 per cent of their energies to coping with the neuroses of their wives; and this can hardly produce good work . . ." (But perhaps happy homes, I silently reflected.) Sometimes his night-work struck me as being a flight—from loneliness.

However this may be, he devoted almost all his time to his work. Meanwhile he kept in close touch with the literary and artistic life of Stockholm and countries abroad; he read the important literary news in a number of languages and —as we later learned—regularly kept a sort of debating diary.

One of his closest friends, Henrik Klackenberg, a member of the Supreme Administrative Court, wrote after his death:

"In attempting a hasty summary of the traits in Dag Hammarskjöld's character that emerged during nearly ten years of our work together in the Finance Department, both before and during the war years, I recall a phrase of his, uttered at a moment of deep feeling, about a person dear to him: 'She was rich in the qualities I value most highly: she was brave and good.'

"Brave and good. Such was the moral standard which Dag himself lived up to, to a rare degree.

"It may sound petty of me to use such simple, boy-scout virtues to describe the successful man, world-famous for his brilliant intelligence and constructive, creative capacity. Yet whatever the admiration and respect commanded by his rich personal qualities and outstanding ability, I remember chiefly his moral stature and incorruptible justice, his integrity and whole-hearted commitment, and his never-failing sense of responsibility vis-à-vis the Task. Yet emphasis on these traits should not suggest an external, forbidding morality. On the contrary he had devastating charm. His colleagues readily became his personal friends. But least of all in the portrait of Dag Hammarskjöld should one lose sight of the gently considerate, somewhat diffident friendliness in this singularly live and richly-faceted personality.

"In searching for the keynote of Dag's nature, as I understood it, I grope for some profane-religious concept, such as the motto with which Karin Boye gave life and meaning to in our generation: Trust, Reliance, Good Will."

Such was his impact on his closest colleagues. But under that ever-engaging exterior there were depths of unease, even dread. He was a very good dissembler, but he felt that he was beginning to function more and more like a perfect machine—and every day he had to talk "baby-talk" with those about him.

The situation became especially irksome when he started to work closely with the Swedish social-democratic Government. A curious state of things developed when his conservative old father Hjalmar Hammarskjöld beheld two of his sons, Bo and Dag, as permanent secretaries in the Social and Finance Departments respectively, under social-democratic governments, drawing up almost the whole of the juridical basis for the modern Welfare State of Sweden. It is said that only once during this period did he become grave and silent, and that was when his youngest son took the ministerial oath and thus became a member—albeit unpolitical—of the social-democrat cabinet.

Dag Hammarskjöld made a most subtle attempt to legitimize his position. He wrote an essay, "The Civil Servant and Society": an explanation directed at the many who marveled to witness his collaboration with a party in power with whose basic views he could have little in common.

In this article he stresses first that the civil servant serves the community and no particular group, and that as such he cannot work for his own political ends. "His private political judgment can never outweigh his duty as a civil servant unless he considers that his own view represents a communal interest about which, objectively, there can be no two opinions." But above all it was Hammarskjöld's belief that by virtue of expert knowledge the experienced civil servant could, anonymously and invisibly, influence current policy. A "strongly political feeling" could change the situation within the administrative milieu and influence the outcome, without entailing any deviation from objectivity on the part of the permanent official. The personal convictions of the expert might exert a tacit influence upon developments "through the opportunity for free criticism in discussion with members of the party in power": an opportunity ever open to him.

When Hammarskjöld became Secretary-General of the United Nations he adapted this basic principle with consistency and great skill.

He ended the article quoted above by outlining the consequences of this principle. He wrote:

"One of [its] first products . . . is a respect for historical practice, built up through generations of effort and of attempts to find solutions to problems. Here we encounter a markedly conservative feature. Another result is that political actions will be governed by respect for the individual, which may result on the one hand in the greatest possible liberty for him to shape his life as he chooses, and on the other in social justice in the form of equal rights and equal opportunity for all. It is on this latter point that liberal and social-radical elements find common ground. Finally the ethic exemplified by Schweitzer finds expression in the subordination of private interests to the whole: a moral obligation firstly to the community, in the sense of nation; secondly to that larger community represented by internationalism. This view, in all its modes of expression, is bound to be characterized by a respect for the convictions of others which is difficult to reconcile with the brilliant one-sidedness of the born party-man.

"To the superficial observer this blend of conservative, liberal, social-radical and internationalistic elements may appear eclectic in the extreme. If so, it is because he fails to see that these elements have not been dragged together from different directions, but have grown out of the same basic view which, so far from indicating any desire to have a finger in every pie, or an inability to choose, leads on the contrary to having no home in any political party, owing to the consistency with which the individual attitude to life is reflected in the political sphere."

Hammarskjöld gained more and more adherents and colleagues. And became more and more solitary.

It was then he fled into the wilderness: to the

mountains and to esoteric poetry. He seems to have felt especially drawn towards what was difficult—as if he had to master the toughest linguistic and philosophical problems before he could properly appreciate a writer. During these years he was somber. I know this from his letters. "For all of us, no doubt, existence acquires an increasing chill as we grow older," he wrote to me at the age of twenty-eight. And went on:

"To 'go one's own way' *now* means surely more than ever to go that way alone. The common aims, the staked-out path, are quite certainly no more than wishful dreaming for any of us. Of course one can run with the herd and find warmth among others, but can this be done without sacrificing what is more important? In a way one can envy Nazi Youth: according to their conception of the ideal, the path of the group coincides with that of the individual, as in the early days of the Workers' Movement. It all sounds very fine when Nietzsche says: '*Den Weg* kann ich nicht, dieser aber ist der meine' ('I cannot go *that* way; *this* one is mine')—so long as one ignores the disruption of community-life that this implies.

"I've rambled on about this merely to give you the grounds for my conclusion: we can't afford to lose anything we hold in common just because of the conflicts that chance arranges for us."

Certainly I admired and revered him. But he

was so different from me. He had lived so sheltered a life; his only (apparent) problem was his attachment to his mother. He seemed to me quite ignorant of all that I had known: the threat of death for many years, the tempestuous experience of women, encounters with the sordid, and the continual handicap of fever and poverty. I always listened most attentively to what he said; I thought he spoke very sensibly and well-advisedly. Yet he spoke as through a pane of glass. It often seemed to me that that pane would never be smashed unless he fell in love with a really impossible, charming, selfish woman, or became mortally ill, or encountered a series of undeserved set-backs. Until that happened he would always seem to me—despite his perfections—in some way lifeless.

I wrote a new novel which was praised by the critics, but which in fact was poor; it was done far too hastily. Dag Hammarskjöld wrote me a letter—which made a strong impression on me— in which he explained what was wrong with it.

"Some pages are so inspired with your 'furia' that nobody could fail to rejoice at your success in giving full expression to your most personal emotions; and if my final judgment is that even so you didn't give all that you might have, it's because so many decisive episodes are portrayed with less than the vivid seriousness of which you're capable. You must certainly be well aware of this yourself, and I'm quite unqualified to judge of literary merit. I take just one example: the scene in bed lacks any literary justification unless presented with such steely psychological truth and with such—may I say—tenderness in its treatment of the human aspect of that wretchedness as to raise it to the level of a symbol of humanity in general. You, an admirer of *Point Counter Point*, should understand what I mean. Of course you may object that the scene has its appointed place in the construction of the novel, but this is insufficient excuse for an inadequate presentation—especially if that scene is not unique in aim and quality. The sex-motif must not be treated in psychologically inadequate and banal terms if it is to be given its due place in cultural life. And you have already clearly shown your ability to reach a high level in this sphere. A harder look and gentler hands next time! You may remember Conrad's characteristic phrase: 'To live up to the standard by which you are credited by your friends.' "

This was Dag at his best. For me the letter was salutary: it showed me more clearly than any of the reviews the inadequacy of my book; it showed me that no one—however goaded by lack of money—can write a novel on a theme beyond his powers in twelve days, with impunity. I began to have an inkling of the demands that Dag made upon those he accepted as his friends.

Yet in the tenderness of his heart he became

uneasy lest he had spoken too harshly, and a few days later he wrote:

"A day or two ago I was talking to one of my friends, and criticized your book as I did in my letter to you. He stood up for the passages in question, but added: 'You must admit that the basis of your criticism is that in your heart you have staked so much of yourself on Stolpe.' This reply was wholesomely revealing."

All this seemed to me rather too soulful, and I put away the troubled letters without properly reflecting on them. By this time I had experienced many things that Dag had not encountered: the threat of death, evil in human shape, brutal selfishness in pathological form. Therefore I considered Dag inexperienced, and myself in no real need of his counsel. I was fighting for dear life in the den of lions, uncertain of the outcome —and up there on the safe marble bench sat the perfect gentleman giving me good advice. Such was my somewhat bitter summary.

In fact I was very stupid. I ought rather to have clung to him more than to any other in my generation, and not released a single side of me that he did not approve.

Dag Hammarskjöld's romanticism about mountains, his enthusiasm for esoteric poetry and cryptic philosophers, seemed at times like a sort of escapism. He lived intensively in his work, but he never had a home in the ordinary sense of the word. He could talk very practically about these things; he once compared himself to a Catholic priest who renounces marriage in order to give his love to all. Success notwithstanding, he remained, during the years before his great vocation, dominated by the same unrest as before, well-disciplined though it may have been. It was as if, for all his intelligence, loyalty and comradeship, he was living somehow *alongside* life.

In 1936 when I attempted to draw him into a certain group of Christian workers, he replied: "I envy you, if you possess what you believe you possess. But so far it is in a more hidden community that I seek the innermost reality of life."

If one asked him what he really wanted to be, when his job as peerless second fiddle in the administration came to an end, he would look bleak and reply that there was little choice. Perhaps a lord-lieutenant, like his father.

Chapter 5

OF HAMMARSKJÖLD's professional colleagues not one knew him; this is evident from their memorial articles. Many persisted in denying that he was interested in religion at all, or could be described as a Christian. He went regularly to church, not only in Stockholm, as was natural, but also during his New York period, when he alternated between Protestant, Greek Orthodox and above all Catholic places of worship; but he never talked about it. Even less did he try to proselytize.

Not until his diary was published did it become clear to everyone that there had been another Dag Hammarskjöld besides the suave diplomat, the expert, the tough mountain-climber, the learned book-collector: namely, a Christian mystic.

Although during that time I knew him less well, I myself never heard him discuss anything but religious problems, whether on the stage, in literature or in reality. Clearly he became a different person according to his company.

On reading his book one is astonished to find that—in a quiet way—he could be a terrifying satirist. He sketches type after type of those about him, and notes their imperfections.

He heard the screech of gulls on a May evening. He scans the sky for the bird: "Only when I get quite close does he impel himself a few yards to one side with an indolent flap of his wings—a well-nourished carrion bird who feels so much at home among us all."

One can be sure that he knew many such carrion birds; he used to point them out especially among unscrupulous reporters of the more sensational press, whom Verner von Heidenstam, the Nobel laureate, once called the "rag-tag and bob-tail of the spirit."

Here is another arresting portrait from his diary:

"He was impossible. It wasn't that he didn't attend to his work: on the contrary, he took endless pains over the tasks he was given. But his manner of behavior brought him into conflict with everybody and, in the end, began to have an adverse effect on everything he had to do with.

"When the crisis came and the whole truth had to come out, he laid the blame on us: in his conduct there was nothing, absolutely nothing to reproach. His self-esteem was so strongly bound up, apparently, with the idea of his innocence, that one felt a brute as one demonstrated, step by step, the contradictions in his defence and, bit by bit, stripped him naked before his own eyes. But justice to others demanded it.

"When the last rag of a lie had been taken from him and we felt there was nothing more to be said, out it came with stifled sobs.

" 'But why did you never help me? Why didn't you tell me what to do? You knew that I always felt you were against me. And fear and insecurity drove me further and further along the course you now condemn me for having taken. It's been so hard—everything. One day, I remember, I was so happy: one of you said that something I had produced was quite good—'

"So, in the end, we were, in fact, to blame. We had not voiced our criticisms, but we had allowed them to stop us from giving him a single word of acknowledgement, and in this way had barred every road to improvement.

"For it is always the stronger one who is to blame. We lack life's patience. Instinctively, we try to eliminate a person from our sphere of responsibility as soon as the outcome of this particular experiment by Life appears, in our eyes, to be a failure. But Life pursues her experiments far beyond the limitations of our judgment. This is also the reason why, at times, it seems so much more difficult to live than to die."

This self-searching is moving. But we must own that it was also needful. Before Hammarskjöld's break-through he had a tendency to appoint himself judge: to look *down* on people—however kindly. He and I had one brief conflict in our youth, resulting from sheer misunderstanding over a trifle. When I heard that he had spoken patronizingly of my motives I called upon him and spoke my mind. He went deathly white. And when he rang up later to explain, I put down the receiver. At last he wrote a pleading letter, not merely to apologize but to beg sincerely and humbly for "forgiveness." When we later met at the house of his tearful mother, who had taken this childish row in deadly earnest, he said—according to my diary—"Did you see how mummy was crying? I tell you I did the same thing when you wanted to break with me. You're so stormy inside that ordinary people can't cope . . ."

After this we were better friends than ever. I had seen his temptation to play the demigod, but also his humble readiness to beg for forgiveness when he'd made a mistake.

In fact it is impossible to utter any criticism of Dag Hammarskjöld which he himself has not phrased far more sharply in his diary. He whips himself with scorpions.

I believe none of his friends had any idea of this side to him.

"Praise nauseates you—but woe betide him who does not recognize your worth."

* * *

"If you don't speak ill of others more often than you do, this certainly isn't from any lack of desire. But you know that malice only gives you elbowroom when dispensed in carefully measured doses."

* * *

"You are your own god—and are surprised when you find that the wolf pack is hunting you across the desolate ice fields of winter."

* * *

"When all becomes silent around you, and you recoil in terror—see that your work has become a flight from suffering and responsibility, your unselfishness a thinly disguised masochism; hear, throbbing within you, the spiteful, cruel heart of the steppe wolf—do not then anaesthetize yourself by once again calling up the shouts and horns of the hunt, but gaze steadfastly at the vision until you have plumbed its depths."

These notes date from the critical years 1941–1942, when Hammarskjöld was making a career for himself but had not yet found his true direction.

If we want to follow the growth of Christian mysticism in his inner life we must also learn about his demons.

"At any rate, your contempt for your fellow human beings does not prevent you, with a well-guarded self-respect, from trying to win their respect."

*   *   *

"The feeling of shame over the previous day . . . It is not the repeated mistakes, the long succession of petty betrayals—though, God knows, they would give cause enough for anxiety and self-contempt—but the huge elementary mistake, the betrayal of that within me which is greater than I—in a complacent adjustment to alien demands."

I recognize the phrase "that within me which is greater than I" from our talks together in our youth. It is closely akin to the words of Paul Claudel, a favorite writer of his: "that in me which is more myself than I am."

Dag was early aware of this inner voice. For a long time it merely troubled and tormented him. At last he heard its call, and followed. But many painful years—painful despite worldly success—were to pass before he achieved final clarity.

"Do you really have 'feelings' any longer for anybody or anything except yourself—or even that?"

"Does he sacrifice himself for others, *yet for his own sake*—in megalomania?"

More commonplace demons would pop up at times: he was not too superior to feel a faint attraction to the ignoble.

"As a climber you will have a wide sphere of activity even after, if that should happen, you reach your goal. You can, for instance, try to prevent others from becoming better qualified than yourself."

He began to perceive that his life was sterile, and that he used "work as an anaesthetic against loneliness, books as a substitute for people—!" That he was coquettish even in recording his own coquetry. He saw and acknowledged in himself evil forces such as solipsism, lust for power and destructiveness, and he knew that their only conqueror was love. But where was love in his life—except on his tongue? With no one did he have a warm relationship. "It is better for the health of the soul to make one man good than to 'sacrifice oneself for mankind' ", he writes. But where was this one man? "Greedy for honours," "joyless," "killer of joy"—three epithets he gave himself, and not without cause.

> Choked by its clown's mask
> And quite dry, my mind
> Is crumbling.

So he wrote in a poem as late as 1958.

His greatest problem was isolation, loneliness. I believe that nowhere in Swedish literature have I heard a more moving lament over the hopeless isolation of the soul than from this popular, admired and well-loved man. "We reach out to the Other. In vain—for we have never dared to give ourselves."

He tries to rationalize his friendlessness:

"Perhaps a great love is never returned. Had it been given warmth and shelter by its counterpart in the Other, perhaps it would have been hindered from ever growing to maturity. It 'gives' us nothing. But in its world of loneliness it leads us up to summits with wide vistas—of insight." This is dangerous reasoning, and it cannot hide the underlying anguish. In one black moment he wrote with terrible sincerity:

"Your pleasure in yourself does not bloom unsheltered. The commandments are simple: never attach yourself to anyone, and therefore never let anyone in to you! The 'I,' in its efforts to protect its self-delight, throws a ring of cold about itself, which slowly eats into the core . . ."

These lines hint at an appalling inner process of withering and emotional freezing. He began to speculate as to the possibility of "acquiring the right to life in a transcendental co-inherence." And he added: "But doesn't [this] choice call for the kind of faith which moves mountains?"

He wrote once, hauntingly:

"What I ask for is absurd: that life shall have a meaning.

"What I strive for is impossible: that my life shall acquire a meaning.

"I dare not believe, I do not see how I shall ever be able to believe: that I am not alone."

He had still not discovered, though he must long have sensed, that not even the friendless person stands entirely alone, and that at his side he has a higher friend. Contrary to his usual practice he gives day and year—29 July 1958—for the following maxim, so he must have felt it to be of special importance:

"Didst Thou give me this inescapable loneliness so that it would be easier for me to give Thee all?"

In other words he was beginning to suspect that in this his greatest torment there was a purpose—in loneliness he was to be trained for some great future task which without such suffering he would be unable to master.

He looks realistically at the problems of loneliness—of the lonely body too. The following analysis takes one far into his self-knowledge:

"For him who has responded to the call of the Way of Possibility, loneliness may be obligatory. Such loneliness, it is true, may lead to a communion closer and deeper than any achieved by the union of two bodies, but your body is not going to let itself be fobbed off by a bluff: whatever you deny it, in order to follow this call, it will claim back if you fail, and claim back in forms which it will no longer be in your power to select."

Discreetly but honestly he touches here and elsewhere on the lonely person's sexual problems:

> Denied any outlet
> The heat transmuted
> The coal into diamonds.

He wrote that as late as 1959. But he also knew that at times this high pressure was too great. If he spared himself, defeat was near. Another verse runs:

> Because it never found a mate
> Men called
> The unicorn abnormal.

Just how dangerous were the areas he moved in—though sure-footed and led always by his will and his radiant idealism—appears from one of the most remarkable entries in his diary, where an unnamed friend is mentioned. Each word of it should be carefully pondered.

"X— outwardly restless, inwardly ascetic, in feeling anti-feminine. Concordant aspects of a single personality, but without any causal connection between them. While 'more normal' types, when they venture out under the open sky, drag along with them the atmosphere of the office and the bedroom, in his company you can escape into a world of freedom and reality even within thick walls or under a low ceiling. His touch is light, but more unerring and sensitive than that of others. An inflection of his voice can bind, a glance unite.

"My friend, the Popular Psychologist, is certain of his diagnosis. And has understood nothing, nothing."

This is the subtle problem of the solitary. The commentary is so compressed that only with difficulty can one resolve it into logical, clear statement:

"Spiritual liberation has its sensual component, just as claustrophobia of the soul has its physical symbolism and physiological ground."

What is meant here, I think, is that a soul called by God but not yet able to interpret the call, which demands sacrifice and solitude, tries to rationalize its oppressive loneliness by substitute solutions.

It is typical that when the call is understood, all this vanishes like a mist from sunlit fields.

Hammarskjöld probably abstained from physical union with another person. He once made the following entries in his diary, which are of essential importance in the context:

"So rests the sky against the earth. The dark, still tarn in the lap of the forest. As a husband embraces his wife's body in faithful tenderness, so the bare ground and trees are embraced by the still, high light of the morning.

"I feel an ache of longing to share in this embrace, to be united and absorbed. A longing like carnal desire, but directed towards earth, water, sky, and returned by the whispers of the trees, the fragrance of the soil, the caresses of the wind, the embrace of water and light. Content? No, no, no—but refreshed, rested—while waiting."

One should compare this description of desire which turns towards nature, since it may not turn to a woman, with these words:

"The ultimate surrender to the creative act—it is the destiny of some to be brought to the threshold of this in the act of sacrifice rather than the sexual act; and they experience a thunderclap of the same dazzling power."

Both in form and content this is one of Hammarskjöld's most unforgettable maxims. In these few lines are summed up his whole personality-problem, his whole vocation. Not until he brings the word "sacrifice" into the argument does the problem become clear.

Into this proud but somewhat sterile world which I have tried to clarify there suddenly fell a blaze of sunlight. By this light Dag Hammarskjöld recognized himself for the first time, beheld his destiny and understood his calling.

Before I explain what now took place in Hammarskjöld's spiritual life, I think I should quote a criticism written by Dr. John Lindberg, economist and political writer, and published in *Look* magazine. Lindberg knew Hammarskjöld during their student years, and had many heated discussions with him. Lindberg disapproved of Hammarskjöld's association with the social-democratic government, as he considered the association immoral. Their conversation concerned "the relationship between the state and the individual and especially the sovereignty of the human conscience." Lindberg—also a most gifted man—thought he saw in Hammarskjöld a boundless arrogance and a large measure of ruthlessness.

"Hammarskjöld demanded blind submission, and his hardness towards helpless people repelled me more than any other trait in him. How much of this hardness arose from 'a sense of duty' and how much from sheer greed for power? In his diary he betrays his longing for death and talks of a masochistic streak—a trait very rarely seen without its complement of sadism."

Lindberg compares Hammarskjöld with Lawrence of Arabia. "The psychological background, the brilliance, the bent, the ambitions and passions, driven by a burning will, are the same. So is the mask they wore: the aloofness, cruelty, lust for power. Lawrence found his path away from this lust by hiding, withdrawing from the world; Hammarskjöld found it in a self-destructive Messiah-role."

In the 1940s Lindberg still had the same unpleasant impression of him:

"I saw those steel-cold eyes under their haughty arches and could not imagine the man defending a friend or espousing a cause unless it was compatible with his 'duty' to his career. Subsequent changes and myth-making should not blind us to the man's arrogance and conceit. His lust for power forged him into its tool; he had an almost limitless contempt for his fellow-men, yet in return demanded their respect."

Lindberg ended his article by questioning whether Hammarskjöld was entirely accountable for his actions.

I shall not make a detailed reply to this criticism, which seems to be wholesome and salutary amid so many eulogies and sentimental myths. I may add that some of the traits mentioned caused me to withdraw from Hammarskjöld towards the end of the thirties. Yet the criticism covers only one side of the man; Hammarskjöld himself never lost sight of his demons and in the end he conquered them.

Chapter 6

In 1953 he received the call to be Secretary-
General of the United Nations. Earlier, when his
painter-friend Bo Beskow had suggested the idea
to him, Hammarskjöld replied that no one in his
senses would offer him such a post. But the offer
came, and after thinking it over for a short time
he accepted, well aware of his own inadequacy.
He considered the matter not by his father's sick-
bed, as legend has it, but while sitting for his
portrait in Bo Beskow's studio and sipping a glass
of sherry. Once he had accepted he was a
changed man. He wrote to his friend and former
chief, the able, great-hearted Ernst Wigforss, the
social-democratic finance-minister, that he was
now a perfectly happy man: words which I believe he would never have used before—unless
possibly high up on a Swedish mountain. He
now entered upon a task for which the whole of
his peculiar, or at any rate unusual, training had
been the ideal preparation. He was free of anything that hampers and binds most people: fam-

ily life or close emotional ties. He often wrote of the cool sphere of friendship, which gives less than that of love but leaves one freer. He perceived clearly that he would never be able to function as he afterwards did if he had felt obliged to devote his best powers, his tenderest attention and deepest feelings to a family.

However that may be, he found his ideal function, he gave it his whole heart and strength—and suddenly he was free. One could see it in his eyes, which now lost the shyness and reserve so noticeable in his youth, and gained directness and warmth. For the first time, in fact, he was aware of his own stature, and everything about him—energy, will to work, loyalty, character, celibacy, solitude—worked together for the good.

Nothing will be said here of his work in New York. The whole world knows of his contribution in different parts of the globe: the American airmen, whom he succeeded in getting released from imprisonment,* the Suez crisis, the Congo crisis—to mention only the greatest tasks. It soon

---

* The release of the prisoners is a singular story. After vain negotiations in Peking Hammarskjöld returned to New York. A Chinese diplomat in Stockholm heard from a friend of Hammarskjöld that Dag was returning to Sweden to celebrate his fiftieth birthday, and asked what Hammarskjöld would like as a birthday-present. The wise friend replied: books, Chinese paintings, but preferably the American air-

appeared that the U.N. statutes allowed a very free interpretation of the Secretary-General's function. Hammarskjöld proved to be not at all the neutral bureaucratic machine that the Russians may have hoped and believed when they gave him their vote. As we have seen he had long pondered the duties and potentialities of a civil servant. Now he made bold—often without any formal mandate—to pursue extremely energetic and often secret policies of his own. He frequently turned up at trouble-spots and gathered impressions long before the Security Council had had time to meet. With his exceptional flexibility and psychological skill—in this he far surpassed his great father—he could make contacts which no one else would have believed possible, and therefore envisage solutions which others would never have thought of. He wrote to his friend Bo Beskow:

"Suez was my third child. Its parents arrived here in a state of great perplexity and some fury. God knows how it will go—but the baby isn't screaming so much now, and perhaps, with good help, I shall be able to teach it to walk . . . Tragi-comedy in three acts. Act I: Secretary-General as Chaperone (that stage now over). Act II: Secretary-General shows inclination to

---

men. Two days after his birthday Hammarskjöld received the news that the prisoners had been released.

appear as (an ever so respectable) Pimp (this act still unwritten). Act III: Secretary-General—if he's lucky—may try his hand at midwifery . . ."

From another letter to the same man, the following lines give some idea of his mastery of style:

"China was a fantastic experience, and since then I am somehow maturer than before. It was splendid and harrowing, infinitely remote and yet infinitely real. This applies to both the country (landscape), the atmosphere in Peking (that magnificent camp of the nomad princes who came down from the desert across the narrow mountain range—a camp with endlessly repeated rhythms of weighted tent-roofs) and Chou en Lai himself (with a brain of steel, blood on his hands, stern self-discipline and a very warm smile)."

At first he reaped nothing but success. His compatriots felt proud of him; he was elected to the Swedish Academy and there delivered his noted speech on his father. Having no family he found time for intensive literary work. He became a good friend of St. John Perse and translated the latter's work, *Chronique;* it was owing to Hammarskjöld that the Frenchman was awarded the Nobel prize for literature. He became increasingly attracted to the most difficult, most recondite literary works, and in collaboration with his friend the theatre-director Karl

Ragnar Gierow he translated Djuna Barnes's play *Växelsången* (Antiphonal Song). Without Hammarskjöld's help the Dramatiska Theatre of Stockholm could not have obtained the unprinted, posthumous plays of Eugene O'Neill, which were in the widow's possession. Hammarskjöld collected rare editions and works of art, he was interested in music, and even during the New York period was able to play an active part in the Swedish Tourist Association in his own country. Everything seemed to be going well for him; the world admired him, his colleagues looked up to him, and he won the increasing confidence of the statesmen of the world. But behind this renown, this success, this apparently harmonious life, an inner development was taking place, of which the torments—one is tempted to say terrors—were unsuspected by anyone until the posthumous publication of his diary.

Year after year Hammarskjöld introduced his diary with the same quotation: "Night is drawing nigh—" He did this in 1953, the year of his appointment to the United Nations. "For all that has been—Thanks! / To all that shall be—Yes!" Now suddenly, unhesitatingly, he speaks about God. He has made contact with a mighty hand whose grasp he had before evaded.

"When in decisive moments—as now—God acts, it is with a stern purposefulness, a Sophoclean irony. When the hour strikes, He takes what is His. What have *you* to say?—Your prayer has been answered . . . God has a use for you, even though what He asks doesn't seem to suit you at the moment. God, who 'abases him whom He raises up'."

* * *

"It *did* come—the day when the grief became small." That is, when the problem of his isolation ceased to be felt by him as suffering. "For what had befallen me and seemed so hard to bear became insignificant in the light of the demands which God was now making."

* * *

"Not I, but God in me."

On the decisive day itself, 7 April 1953, he quotes from Thomas (not Aquinas, as the Swedish critics—utterly at a loss—imagined, but Kempis):

" 'They that are grounded and established in God can by no means be proud. And they that attribute to God whatsoever good they have received, seek not glory from one another, but the glory which is from God only . . .' "

All at once he is speaking a new language: that of Christian mysticism: "I am the vessel. The draught is God's. And God is the thirsty one." He ponders the word sacrifice. What does it mean? Or the word gift? "He who has nothing can give nothing. The gift is God's—to God."

The remarkable thing is that as soon as his

vocation is clear to him he knows that "the Way ends on the Cross." Everyone, he says, "who has surrendered to it" [i.e., his destiny] knows the truth of this.

On 26 September 1957, another critical date in his life, he notes:

" 'The best and most wonderful thing that can happen to you in this life, is that you should be silent and let God work and speak.'

"Long ago, you gripped me, Slinger. *Now* into the storm. *Now towards your target.*"

All is now sure: "Salty and wind-swept, but warm and glittering. Keeping in step with the measure under the fixed stars of the task." "So—in the self-forgetfulness of concentrated attention—the door opens for you into a pure, living intimacy."

Throughout his youth and the early years of his manhood, Hammarskjöld—like all lonely idealists—had striven to shape and polish his personality towards perfection. This is humanism: faith in mankind. Now he sees—and rejoices with his soul at the discovery—that this battle is not the essential one. He becomes "strong and free, because he no longer exists."

I know little of Dag Hammarskjöld's reading, as for instance when it was that he began to study the great mystics. I have been strongly moved by the effect they had on his spiritual life. In *British Weekly* he once wrote:

"The two ideals that dominated my childhood world were fully congenial and well-suited to the demands made by the world of today, in Albert Schweitzer's ethic, where the ideal of service is borne up by and supports the basic attitude to mankind as set forth in the gospels. But the explanation of how a man may lead a life in active service to the community, while remaining in complete harmony with himself as a member of a spiritual brotherhood, I found in the writings of the great mediaeval mystics: those for whom self-surrender had become the way to self-realisation, and who in 'singleness of mind' and 'inwardness' had found strength to say Yes to every claim made upon them by their neighbor's need; to say Yes also to all that their destiny had in store for them when they fulfilled their duty as they saw it. Love—that much misused, much misunderstood word—meant for them simply an overflowing of the strength that filled them when they lived in true self-forgetfulness, and this love found expression in unhesitating fulfilment of duty and an unreserved acceptance of life, whatever it might bring them personally of toil, suffering—or happiness.

"I know that these discoveries of the laws both for our inner life and our active life have not lost their significance."

He had read St. John of the Cross, and wrote: "—'en una noche oscura.' The Dark Night of the Soul—so dark that we may not even look for faith. The night in Gethsemane when the last friends left you have fallen asleep, all the others are seeking your downfall, and *God is silent*, as the marriage is consummated."

Hammarskjöld soon imposed this stern doctrine on himself, knowing from the beginning what would be demanded of him. "The unheard-of—to be in the hands of God" impelled him to write:

Give me a pure heart—that I may see Thee,
A humble heart—that I may hear Thee,
A heart of love—that I may serve Thee,
A heart of faith—that I may abide in Thee.

* * *

"It is not sufficient to place yourself daily under God. What really matters is to be *only* under God: the slightest division of allegiance opens the door to daydreaming, petty conversation, petty boasting, petty malice—all the petty satellites of the death-instinct.

"The third hour. And the ninth.—They are *here*. And *now*. They *are* now!

" 'Jesus will be in agony even to the end of the world. We must not sleep during that time.' (*Pascal*)

"We must not— And for the watcher is the far-off present—also present in his contact with

mankind among whom, at every moment, Jesus
dies in someone who has followed the trail marks
of the inner road to the end:

> love and patience,
> > righteousness and humility,
> faith and courage,
> stillness."

With Eckhardt he knows that: " 'God has
never given Himself, and never will, to a will
alien to His own: where He finds His will, He
gives Himself.' "

Among the French writers who spoke with
special force to Dag Hammarskjöld, Paul Claudel
was one. Dag writes in his notebook: "The
Lover desires the perfection of the Beloved—
which requires, among other things, the liberation of the Beloved from the Lover."

This summarizes the thematic problem of
Claudel's great play *Le Soulier de Satin*, in which
Don Rodrigue and Doña Prouhèze, who can
never forget their love for each other, yet de-
prive themselves of the possibility of living together.

In this play are many scenes in which I now
always seem to see Dag Hammarskjöld. The
Spanish king chooses Don Rodrigue to be viceroy of America. Why? "What I must have is a

man who can never be stifled; I must have such a fire that it instantly consumes all the temptations that come its way—like straw!" The king adds, "Yes, if he had not tested this love himself I should have had to test it by inflicting on him some great injustice." That is to say that the condottiere is ripe for his historical task in the world because the beloved, whom he can never win, has lit a fire within him: a fire so insatiable that nothing on earth can quench it.

Dag Hammarskjöld probably never knew such a renunciation of a single beloved woman—but he sacrificed his whole life; he paid the price of a lifelong, painful, humiliating isolation, and for that very reason was able to shoulder the burden of world-responsibility. At the moment of his decision he felt that the pressure had lifted and that he was free.

It is interesting to study his image of Christ, in whom he sees "a young man, adamant in his commitment, who walks the road of possibility to the end without self-pity or demand for sympathy, fulfilling the destiny he has chosen—even sacrificing affection and fellowship when the others are unready to follow him—into a new fellowship." He always emphasizes Christ's solitude and finds a pattern in it. "As I continued along the Way, I learned, step by step, word by word, that behind every saying in the Gospels stands *one* man and *one* man's experience. Also behind the prayer that the cup might pass from him, and his promise to drink it. Also behind each of the words from the Cross."

It has been said that Dag Hammarskjöld identified himself with Christ in a blasphemous way. I shall discuss this point later. Here I would only stress that he very early discovered that he was never intended to be released from his loneliness: it was loneliness that was his vocation.

Chapter 7

THERE WAS another theme in Dag Hammar-
skjöld's philosophy, as essential to it as loneliness;
and that was death.

Though I fancied I knew something about his
other ideas, I own that it was through his diary
that I first understood how central a role the
theme of death played in his life.

One of his favourite authors was Joseph Conrad. He especially loved *Lord Jim*.

This book, it will be remembered, ends with
the scene where Lord Jim, that singular adven-
turer, who has accepted responsibility for a great
disaster that overtook his companions, and especially for the death of the son of his powerful
friend Doramin through a treacherous attack,
faces Doramin calmly and without attempting to
defend himself, convinced that he has acted
rightly and been true to himself—but also certain that no one will understand him:

"Doramin, struggling to keep his feet, made,

with his two supporters, a swaying, tottering group; his little eyes stared with an expression of mad pain, of rage, with a ferocious glitter, which the bystanders noticed; and then, while Jim stood stiffened and with bared head in the light of torches, looking him straight in the face, he clung heavily with his left arm round the neck of a bowed youth, and lifting deliberately his right, shot his son's friend through the chest.

"The crowd, which had fallen apart behind Jim as soon as Doramin had raised his hand, rushed tumultuously forward after the shot. They say that the white man sent right and left at all those faces a proud and unflinching glance. Then, with his hand over his lips he fell forward, dead."

Dag Hammarskjöld was not only Rodrigue the viceroy; he was Lord Jim, calmly and proudly standing to await a senseless death—because he had done the right thing.

Of this scene, one of the greatest in the art of the novel, Hammarskjöld writes in his book:

" 'At the frontier of the unheard-of—' The unheard-of—perhaps this simply refers to Lord Jim's last meeting with Doramin, when he has attained absolute courage and humility in an absolute loyalty to himself. Conscious of guilt, but at the same time conscious of having atoned, so far as atonement is possible in life—by what he has done for those who are now asking for his life.

Untroubled and happy. Like someone wandering by himself along a lonely sea-shore."

I shall never be able to read that final scene in *Lord Jim* without remembering Dag Hammarskjöld, flung out of his aircraft in the Congo, still alive for a few minutes, leaning against a rock—in absolute fidelity to himself and his calling.

But for him death had a quite special fascination, somewhat different from the attraction towards death of which one finds so many examples in literature.

He once wrote:

"Your body must become familiar with its death—in all its possible forms and degrees—as a self-evident, imminent, and emotionally neutral step on the way towards the goal you have found worthy of your life."

He never wanted to heroize or romanticize death:

"As an element in the sacrifice, death is a fulfillment, often it is a degradation, and it is never an elevation."

Towards the end of his life Hammarskjöld was haunted by strange premonitions of death. Some of these he captured in poems. He saw himself as a gladiator in the Roman arena, trapped at last in the net. Or:

I have watched the others:
Now I am the victim,

Strapped fast to the altar
For sacrifice.

Dumb, my naked body
Endures the stoning, dumb
When slit up and the live
Heart is plucked out.

This poem was finished in the spring of 1961.
In another he stands against a target, nailed to
it by the first arrows:

What have I to fear?
If their arrows hit,
If their arrows kill,
What is there in that to cry about?

Others have gone before,
Others will follow.

On 18 June 1961 he sees himself in yet another
situation. He is being led out between two
guards towards a wall where he is to be shot:

Lean and sunburnt
A little bent,
As if apologizing
For his strength,
His features tense,
But looking quite calm.

Exactly as Hammarskjöld appears in the later photographs where, deathly tired, he is seen inspecting the United Nations forces in the Congo.

The end of the poem takes an unexpected turn:

> When I feel anxious,
> It is not for him.
> Do I feel a compulsion in me
> To be so destroyed?
> Or is there someone
> In the depths of my being,
> Waiting for permission
> To pull the trigger?

Quite certainly there was in the lonely Hammarskjöld a mounting death-wish, which one cannot avoid relating to his last, inexplicable adventure in the Congo, and its attendant, senseless risk.

At times the world's reality faded from his eyes, and another reality, with which he had slowly grown familiar, loomed ahead. This appears in the wonderful poem he entered at the end of his diary, dated 24 August 1961:

> Is it a new country
> In another world of reality
> Than Day's?

Or did I live there
Before Day was?

I awoke
To an ordinary morning with gray light
Reflected from the street,
But still remembered
The dark-blue night
Above the tree line,
The open moor in moonlight,
The crest in shadow.
Remembered other dreams
Of the same mountain country:
Twice I stayed on its summits,
I stayed by its remotest lake,
And followed the river
Towards its source.
The seasons have changed
And the light
And the weather
And the hour.
But it is the same land.
And I begin to know the map
And to get my bearings.

A
Spiritual
Portrait

Chapter 8

THE CURIOUS thing is that, despite all Hammarskjöld's eager discussions, his view of existence and his religious problems, his inner life seems to have been almost entirely unsuspected by even his closest colleagues. He wrote to a friend:

"Where is the human warmth in my life? Everywhere and nowhere. In my case part of the price to pay is no doubt this: that one can devote oneself as unreservedly as possible to one's task only if it can be done without causing the slightest deprivation to anyone else. To be able to die *really*—in the evangelical sense, which is so fearfully realistic as an image of the human condition —we may, in certain situations, be forced into paradoxical egoism ('Who is my Mother and my Brother', etc., etc.?). The substitute for this is the cheerful easy warmth I find in contact with my friends; a sort of comradeship beneath the same star where *one desires nothing and gains so much.*"

His friends did not know him. After Hammarskjöld's death, when I described him in an essay as a Christian mystic, this essay was hailed from many quarters with irony or scorn: how, in de-Christianized Sweden, could Hammarskjöld be anything so despicable as a practising Christian —far less anything so suspect as a Christian mystic?! One of his colleagues, Henrik Klackenberg, a member of the Supreme Administrative Court, who in other respects had produced the finest study of Hammarskjöld's personality and everyday discipline, wrote—among other things —under the heading "Right Denomination?" the following:

"Since his death Dag Hammarskjöld has in certain circles been represented to us as a great churchman. This somewhat surprises me, though in our admiration we may feel inclined to be generous with the designation 'Christian,' and I wonder whether such a claim is justified. It is always difficult to pronounce upon another man's philosophy, and the life of anyone passes through varying phases. Yet during our many years together he never, so far as I know, attended church—except occasionally to accompany his mother—or expressed any need for divine worship. I felt that he had difficulty in tolerating the form of dishonesty characteristic of some modern preachers who, while using a religiously symbolic language, interpolate their own opin-

A Spiritual Portrait

ions, careless whether the congregation interprets their words in another and more literal sense. For Dag, intellectual honesty was a self-evident essential. Yet on the other hand he was not lacking in feeling for and interest in the religious sphere . . . All the same, he had deviated considerably from the pure evangelical-Lutheran doctrine . . ."

These restrainedly scornful words are characteristic. Dag Hammarskjöld himself has answered his friend in the statement previously quoted in Chapter Two about his Christian faith:

"Faith is a state of the mind and the soul. In this sense we can understand the words of the Spanish mystic St. John of the Cross: 'Faith is the union of God with the soul.' The language of religion is a set of formulas which register a basic spiritual experience. It must not be regarded as describing, in terms to be defined by philosophy, the reality which is accessible to our senses and which we can analyse with the tools of logic. I was late in understanding what this meant. When I finally reached that point, the beliefs in which I was once brought up and which, in fact, had given my life direction even while my intellect still challenged their validity, were recognized by me as mine in their own right, and by my free choice. I feel that I can endorse those convictions without any compromise with the demands of that intellectual honesty which is the very key to maturity of mind."

This is a part of Hammarskjöld's article in *British Weekly*, in which he also said: "The explanation of how a man may lead a life in active service to the community, while remaining in *A Spiritual Portrait* complete harmony with himself as a member of a spiritual brotherhood, I found in the writings of the great mediaeval mystics . . . Love—that much misused, misunderstood word—meant for them simply an overflowing of the strength that filled them when they lived in true self-forgetfulness, and this love found expression in unhesitating fulfilment of duty and an unreserved acceptance of life, whatever it might bring them personally of toil, suffering—or happiness." (See page 87.)

This is to say that the Christian faith in which Hammarskjöld was brought up he can now make his own, and confirm (cf. Klackenberg: ". . . he had deviated considerably from the pure evangelical-Lutheran doctrine"!); he adds that this has happened without his having to "compromise the intellectual honesty which is the key to maturity of the soul" (cf. Klackenberg: "For Dag, intellectual honesty was a self-evident essential" —therefore he could not be a professing Christian!)

This example is not unique. When Hammarskjöld's *Vägmärken* (*Markings*) came out, it was a real shock for Sweden to find itself confronted by unequivocally Christian confessions, a living faith in God and Christ, a life which in every respect was subordinated to the claims of holiness. The normal, logical result would have been for the atheistic, anti-Christian press—the predominating one—to repudiate Hammarskjöld's Christianity, and call it perverted, unhealthy, intellectually dishonest, and all the other things that are commonly said of professing Christians in those circles. But Hammarskjöld's radiant influence—and his position—were so strong that there could be no question of the vulgarities that are so gleefully aimed, for instance, at the bishops of Sweden. People went to work in another way.

In the leading evening paper the question was raised whether Hammarskjöld considered himself a new saviour, a new Christ. All the passages in the book which illustrate Hammarskjöld-the-disciple's adherence to his Lord were quoted and exploited, as if Hammarskjöld had wanted to *identify* himself with Christ, and believed that through his self-sacrifice he could save the world!

In *Dagens Nyheter*, the largest national newspaper, there appeared a long article by its anticlerical editor, Olof Lagercrantz, to very much the same effect. Hammarskjöld's role in life was to sacrifice himself for mankind. "He identifies himself more and more with Jesus. His conviction, like this exaltation, increases year by year. He works unnaturally hard, and overstrain must certainly act as the whip that spins the top at mounting speed. In the diary for 1957, Jesus is transformed into a politician . . . During the last years when the Congo policy had led to violent Russian intervention, Hammarskjöld's Jesus-identification found increasingly extravagant expression: 'Nevertheless, not as I will,' he writes in November 1960, in a poem where he sees himself in Gethsemane. 'The torches draw near, and it is time for the Judas kiss and the cross . . .' "

One need perhaps not waste time in countering these observations, which only show how in a half de-Chrisitanised country even the most elementary features of Christian discipleship are unknown, or regarded as presumptuousness or blasphemy.

But in a Danish Christian paper, Denmark's gifted ambassador to Paris, Ejvind Bartels, wrote an article of a different order, of which I must quote the essential passages, partly because, despite its erroneous view, it is psychologically very clear-sighted, and partly because in discussing Bartels I shall have the opportunity to penetrate a little further into Hammarskjöld's Christian mysticism.

"In his book it is not the great economist, the supple diplomat or the man of action that we meet. As Dag Hammarskjöld himself says in his remarkable letter to Leif Belfrage, the book is a record of his discussions with himself—and with God. And it is to be noted that he gives as his motive for publishing it a wish to correct the profile that others drew of him, after he succeeded to the post that Trygve Lie called the most exacting of all. Strange that Hammarskjöld should care what profile other people drew. Strange too that so noble a man should not rather have been thinking about his message. Perhaps he had none.

"The book, as he himself defines it, is a series of trail marks that have guided him in his career, and it reveals in a veiled form his own view of his life and, not least, of his mission.

"Hammarskjöld presents his book as diary-entries, but one may doubt the accuracy of this. There is indeed a certain dating of his thoughts, but the chronology bears all the marks of re-arrangement, and rather than a tracing of developments through time, it gives the effect of a code which must be deciphered before one can understand the text. Thus to appreciate fully the entry for 7 April 1953 it is important to know that this was the date on which he became Secretary-General. Perhaps some of the other 'codes' in the 'diary,' or even all, may be broken in this way.

"Hammarskjöld does not conceal the fact that the book has been so edited; and the work was evidently done before his last journey to the Congo. The letter to Leif Belfrage is characteristically undated; the first words in the book are:

'Only the hand that erases can write the true thing'—a sound view-point, by the way.

"Thus if I were to define Hammarskjöld's book in a few words, I should call it his own myth about his mission.

"What shocks one in the myth is Hammarskjöld's evident belief that, like Christ, he has been chosen by God to be the sacrificial lamb, and that by accepting this destiny he, like Christ, can save mankind. Other critics have already pointed out this blasphemy.

"Hammarskjöld was first and foremost a polished aesthete; and the arranging of the entries has been carried out in such a way that one might wonder whether the book was written by him at all, and is not rather a pastiche—of Hammarskjöld! This doubt is strengthened by the fact that Hammarskjöld's myth about Hammarskjöld had its reassuring confirmation—and its greatness—in that he did in fact meet the end that he had so plainly foreseen. And when this death in the Congo was followed by a buzz of rumors about sabotage and shooting-down, one almost wonders, after reading the myth, whether he did not seek and bring about the death—and make the last entries *after* it!

"This notion expresses the distaste one feels on reading *Markings*.

"Hammarskjöld's was a closed nature with a great need of human contact—and, like Kierkegaard, he loved the pirouette and the double doors. Yet he took care that it should not be too difficult to define the various dance-steps and to open some of the many doors. The following cues—which are his own—seem to me a clear indication of the myth he wanted to establish:

1925–1930   Youth . . . "Thus it was."
1941–1942   "The Middle Years," or time of waiting.
1945–1949   "Towards new shores."
1950–1958   "Night is drawing nigh . . ."

"In 1953, when Hammarskjöld was appointed Secretary-General, there is an addition:

> For all that has been—Thanks!
> To all that shall be—Yes!

"1956–1957. Years when, in the Suez crisis, Hammarskjöld for the first time soaked himself in his mission: 'Before Thee, Father, in righteousness and humility.'

"1958–1959. The years of waiting, before his last mission, in the Congo: 'So shall the world be created each morning anew . . .'

"1961. On Whit Sunday a summary of his mission, ending with an invocation of the cross, and poems which, a fortnight before his death in the Congo, ring with fatalism.

"Hammarskjöld sought exaltation and drained his cup not without a smile.

"But in each and all of these sections of his life, with their appearance of having been written after his death, there are brilliant thoughts, and principles which were those he strove for.

"When only twenty he said in one of his poems that he was:

Ready at any moment to gather everything
Into one simple sacrifice,

and he means that what he can win of life's greatness is reflected in him by his purity. In 1941 and 1942, that is during the first years of the war, there is no word of the world's suffering, only of himself: 'Praise nauseates you—but woe to him who does not recognise your worth.' In 1945 and 1949, when Europe's despairing peace began, come the following thoughts: 'What is one to do on a bleak day but drift for a while through the streets—drift with the stream . . .' and a lightning description of a suicide where he stands by, without courage, thinking only of his aesthetic sadness: '. . . a heroic torso of marble-blonde stone in the soft grass.'

"The years up to 1953 are full of this reflected

self-pity which colors his thoughts, though these are concentrating about the core of the myth: Hammarskjöld's mission: 'Longing— among other things, for the Cross.' In 1951 he touches the Narcissus-legend and the saint's image of 'sun-flame and frost,' and in the same year he gives a coherent sketch of his own destiny as Christ.

"Not until 1953 do we sense stature and strength; the day before his appointment we find the quotation from Thomas à Kempis, stressing his devotion to God and the belief that God has called him. 'The gift is God's—to God.' From this date Hammarskjöld is the chosen one; in the rest of the book he wanted beyond all doubt to describe and dramatize the crescendo in his life of service to mankind, which was to continue after his death and so realize his own myth.

"Typically the writing is of a lyricism that sings of childhood and nature, and—as has been said—it is the Christian dates, Easter and Christmas, that at last liberate his thoughts. Whit Sunday 1961 contains a brief summary of the Hammarskjöld myth, but also the disturbing words: 'But at some moment I did answer *Yes* to Someone or Something,' words that suggest doubt as to his vocation. On 18 June 1961, three months before his death, he wrote a poem portraying the sacrificial lamb:

Or is there someone
In the depths of my being
Waiting for permission
To pull the trigger?

"Though the feeling of distaste mentioned
above lingers in the mind, no one would venture
to deny after reading Hammarskjöld's book that
he seriously sought his way—and found it. It is
also admirable that a man to whom were given
tasks greater perhaps than those borne by any
other Scandinavian of modern times, should have
searched thus, in his God and in himself, the
rock upon which his work was to be founded. I
still doubt whether the apparent blasphemy need
perturb us, for Hammarskjöld could well reply to
his critics that Christianity requires each and all
of us to take up the cross of Christ, and that he,
Hammarskjöld, did it with his eyes open and in
the belief that by so doing he was making the
necessary sacrifice for mankind. The disturbing
thing is not this identification with Christ, which
on the contrary is moving, but in his belief that
he has been singled out, and that his own life
outweighs the suffering of thousands—if not
millions—of others. Therefore the Hammarskjöld myth, despite the sign of the cross, is the
Narcissus myth; and for all the appeals to his

own humility that recur in the book, it is his joy
at his own, bleak destiny that strikes one as the
principal theme. One is even tempted to say that
if Hammarskjöld sought and found death, it was
because this was beautiful to him, 'a heroic torso
of marble-blonde stone in the soft grass.'

"To the question whether Hammarskjöld was
at that time a Christian, the answer according to
his own words can only be yes; nor can there be
any doubt that this discreet aristocrat saw and
explicity affirmed that the precept of Christianity is humanity. Nevertheless I cannot but feel
slight misgivings as to Hammarskjöld's Christian
faith; for there are times when to accept and
even seek death, as self-immolation for mankind,
is, for an unhappy person, the easiest and not the
hardest way out. One may wonder whether
Hammarskjöld perceived that he had been deprived of love for his fellow-man, so that only in
death could he achieve the noblest heights that
were his goal. It is characteristic that Hammarskjöld, as mentioned earlier, in his entry for
Whitsun 1961, talks of a '*Yes* to Someone or
Something' —hardly, then, to a personal God—
and that his references to Christ repeatedly cast a
false light: for to Hammarskjöld Christ was not
the Son of Man who died for our sins. Christ was
Hammarskjöld's forerunner.

"It seems to me difficult to avoid the impression that the great shock of 1953—which others

have called his conversion—is no more than a shock staged by himself, for himself, to create the core of the drama, and that Hammarskjöld, for all his life-long search, remains a pitiful, barren aesthete and intellectual.

"Hammarskjöld's thoughts often resemble Kierkegaard's; the spiritual kinship between the two is evident. In Kierkegaard there was unquestionably a deep and genuine Christian faith, even though—like Hammarskjöld—he had to battle against the contempt of other men. Above all, behind Kierkegaard's many dance-steps there beat a human heart, which I at least seek in vain among Hammarskjöld's notes; remembering always that this may be partly an expression of Hammarskjöld's diffidence, and of his admiration for concise phraseology.

"In the French and Swedish press reference has been made to his affinity with French thought and especially with Pascal, and in one of his entries he quotes Pascal on the death-struggle of Jesus. But there is no spiritual kinship between Hammarskjöld and Pascal. Pascal was a man who broke with the intellectual traditions of centuries, and in his *Pensées* dramatized mankind's choice and search; but the last thing Pascal thought about was himself, and with his robust authority he demolished scholaticism and all human self-centeredness. Hammarskjöld in his book appears far from robust. He is a man who thinks of mankind through himself; one who loves the pallid Christ—who is not ours. One could more properly speak of Hammarskjöld's affinity with Simone Weil who, like him, prepared herself for divine grace—and sought death with Christ.

"My feeling is that the profile Hammarskjöld drew of himself is a feeble one and—while no one could question his intellectual and moral purity—results from his having attempted to span a register beyond his range. He wanted us to believe that behind the schooled diplomat and eminent thinker was a powerful personality, led by God towards a destiny that could be written in the holy book. But he has left the profile of a man whose serious striving we cannot doubt, but who in this strife encountered not victory but defeat. For his death was a flight—what the French so aptly term 'a flight forward'—and a full stop; a full stop to his political activity too, which lacked both supporting strength and roots. It was not, like the death of Christ, a victory and a beginning.

"There remains therefore the memory of a brilliant intelligence, of an aesthete attracted by the exquisite, a disconcerting Narcissus and a despairing Dag Hammarskjöld."

Ambassador Bartels's article attracted much attention in Sweden, and forms one of the most important contributions to the great debate on

Hammarskjöld's posthumous book. I estimate it as a little masterpiece both in style and psychological insight.

Yet my admiration for Bartels's article does not imply agreement. I believe that many of those who were once close to Hammarskjöld, especially in youth, then saw him as the isolated aesthete, cold and self-contemplative, incapable of warmth towards anyone—which tallies well with the image so gracefully drawn by Bartels. But I wonder whether those who knew him in his later years would subscribe to this portrait. Many of us, indeed, can testify to his personal warmth, his ceaseless vigilance on his friends' behalf, his joy when they prospered and his concern when they sank below their proper level. One of his close friends, Karl Ragnar Gierow, the theatre-director and poet, said in a fine memorial speech that he had never met so "light" [in the sense of bright, or luminous] a man as Hammarskjöld. I would stress this: in his *last* years, *after* he found his vocation, he shone. He was borne up by his task.

To be a polished aesthete, to content himself with regarding his own reflection, to enjoy his own isolation, to flee from people to books or to alpine escapism—these things were present in Hammarskjöld, as a temptation. The year before his appointment he appeared very frosty; it was then that he pronounced stern judgment on a number of his colleagues. But we know from many sources that he overcame this temptation. His diary reveals in detail his severe strictures on his own pride, self-centeredness and contempt for mankind. He feared an emotional freeze-up. I must admit that until I read his book I had never dreamt that his isolation was so horrible a torment.

Dag Hammarskjöld was now "called"; that is, he conceived his task as being given him by God. At the same instant he became aware of his destiny, his own painful and singular path: all the asceticism, solitude and training in abstinence now revealed themselves as necessary to enable him to carry out his great work. He saw a meaning not only in this work, but also in the agonizing path he had already had to travel without ever being able to reconcile himself to it. He asked himself how he could ever love, when he never came really close to any other person (for "person" read "woman" if preferred). He now saw—though he never made the comparison—that his purpose was that of St. Francis and other disciples of Christ: to follow the Saviour's own and seemingly lonely way, that their love might suffice for all men. This is no mannered aestheticism, no narcissism in disguise: it is classical Christianity.

Ambassador Bartels, however, is dubious of Hammarskjöld's Christianity. He thinks that

Dag's Christ is not Christianity's Saviour, the Son of Man who died for our sins, but rather a brother who had gone ahead of Hammarskjöld along the same path. Bartels even ventures to speak of Hammarskjöld's "apparent blasphemy," and says that he magnified and dramatized his destiny—which was really no more than a fine-drawn man's thorough defeat as person and politician—into a veritable drama of salvation. Hammarskjöld, he says, identified himself with Christ and saw himself as a saviour-figure who desired to sacrifice himself for mankind through death.

I am certain that this is a wrong interpretation. Hammarskjöld's Christianity cannot be judged by this posthumous book alone. He wrote other manuscripts which sooner or later will come to light, and they give quite a different picture. (Nor need we be surprised that in *Markings* Hammarskjöld makes no reference to his political ideas and experiences.)

Bartels admits to being moved by Hammarskjöld's endeavor to follow the way of Christ, to accept suffering, loneliness and other tortures —among them a very concrete one, which it is still too early to touch upon—and the cross itself. But he is revolted by the idea that Hammarskjöld should consider himself "singled out, and that his own life outweighed the suffering of thousands —if not millions—of others."

Neither in Hammarskjöld's book nor in his letters is there a hint of so naive a blasphemy. He is

chosen in the same way as all Christians who
have been "called" are chosen; there is no more
to it than that. The only difference is that he mi-
nutely examines the implications of this calling,
and finds that true obedience to it entails complete self-surrender. He must endure, without
replying to, the vilification of Herbert Tingsten,
the great publicist, and Khruschchev—to name
the two gentlemen who plagued him most. He
must renounce all idea of personal happiness, and
be content to sacrifice his private life for the sake
of his task. All this is a normal, Christian attitude.
He never over-estimates himself. He is well
aware—as we find especially in some of his
letters—that his policies will not be as successful
as he at first expected (notably after the solution
of the Suez crisis); that one day he may be over-
thrown and cast aside as a thing of no value, and
indeed be killed. The thought of death is much
to the fore in his book. Bartels finds this slightly
"coquettish" and does not shrink from suggest-
ing that Hammarskjöld may even have sought
and brought about his own death. This is a horrible insinuation, for it can only imply Bartels's
acceptance of the possibility that, to achieve a
sacrificial death for himself, Hammarskjöld was
willing to risk the lives of a number of colleagues, or deliberately and cold-bloodedly to sacrifice them too.

This is unthinkable.

When I recall the Dag Hammarskjöld of the last years—warm, loving, open, radiant—I am astonished at Bartel's definition of him as a "pitiful, barren aesthete and intellectual" who "perceived that he had been deprived of love for his fellow-man." The truth—remarkable though it may seem—is the exact opposite: that after finding his vocation Hammarskjöld opened out, burst forth from his armor and made tender, kindly contact even with private individuals, although the dignified diffidence of his nature always remained, as a light and—to me—very charming veil. No, one cannot possibly regard the Hammarskjöld of the last years as "an aesthete attracted by the exquiste, a disconcerting Narcissus and a despairing" man. He had cast off his exquisiteness, and broken with narcissism; he was far from despairing, but rather filled with a new assurance, a new love. Those who knew him can testify to this.

Bartels thinks that Hammarskjöld's death was not "a victory and a beginning," like Christ's. No, it is not to be compared to the Saviour's death: that would be blasphemy indeed. But Hammarskjöld's life and death and posthumous book is, for Sweden, a spiritual event of epoch-making significance. For a decade our fashionable, heathen writers have jeered at any talk of purity, sacrifice, and self-abnegation, as being sheer perversion; and have called Christianity

nonviable and a lie. Parallel with this, our literature has been dragged down to an often porno-
graphic study of people at the sub-human level.
Into this great degradation and poverty Hammarskjöld's book comes like a great light—like a
flood of living, spiritual life—to witness that all
the ancient Christian words may be revivified,
and that the Chrisitan path is still the way of life.

Chapter 9

THERE IS in the diary a passage which has been
much discussed and commented upon, and of
which the content may seem obscure. It runs:

"You asked for burdens to carry—And
howled when they were placed on your shoul-
ders. Had you fancied another sort of burden?
Did you believe in the anonymity of sacrifice?
The sacrificial act and the sacrificial victim are
opposites, and to be judged as such.

"O Caesarea Philippi: to accept condemnation
of the Way as its fulfillment, its definition, to accept this both when it is chosen and when it is
realized."

These words have been interpreted by non-
Christian critics as positive proof that in some
sort of megalomania Hammarskjöld identified
himself with Christ. This of course is not so; to a
dispassionate Christian it has quite a different
sense. If one reads the eighth chapter of St.
Mark's gospel one finds the story of how Jesus

asked his disciples who he was, and was given the answer: "Thou art the Christ." He then forbade them to tell anyone of this. This does not mean that in secret Hammarskjöld fancied himself a Messiah, but that he identified himself with the disciple of Jesus. Then Peter began to warn Jesus of the suffering to come. But Jesus says to the disciples and the people: "Whosoever will come after me, let him deny himself, and take up his cross, and follow me."

Hammarskjöld cries out "O Caesarea Philippi" because in this passage he had vividly perceived that he too, like the disciples, must endure suffering. He expresses this immediately afterwards; he must "accept condemnation as the fruit and fulfilment of the work—to accept it when the work is perceived and when it is chosen." That is, even before starting to serve as a disciple one must accept as an imperative condition the possibility of failure and humiliation. No advancement or success in the superficial sense is to be expected, if the service is to be acceptable to the Lord.

I have dwelt on this point for a particular reason. For the problem is, what was the suffering that Hammarskjöld was experiencing so keenly and indeed sinking under?

No one who saw the tense and, under all his suavity, tormented young administrator in Stockholm could have guessed that he was being prepared for quite a different task. Certainly *he* did not. But when his life reached its dramatic climax, everything in his past took on a deep meaning—including his strict self-training and his apparent escapism, and his way of living life as if he were not living it at all.

With a single stroke he cut himself loose from what the gospel calls "the world."

Yet at the same time he knew from the very beginning that what awaited him was—and had to be—continual misunderstandings and insults. And they came. The Soviet delegates reviled him as being corrupt and dishonest, and even pointed him out as a murderer who had had a finger in the pie when Lumumba was killed by his enemies. Hammarskjöld sat absolutely still during these accusations and replied to them always with great dignity. He was invariably polite to the Russians. Yet those who had known his face well since youth were deeply disturbed to see how it altered during his last months. He was also over-working at this time, and despite his well-known work-discipline he was an exhausted man under great stress when he made his last journey to the Congo. He recognized himself in his father's situation: like Hjalmar Hammarskjöld Dag was now abused and misunderstood. Especially cruel was the sharp criticism fired from Stockholm by the illustrious liberal publicist Herbert Tingsten, whom in many respects he admired.

Hammarskjöld's diary-entries during his last years consist almost entirely of lyrics. Many of these poems are already classics in Swedish literature. In them one can plainly discern his great weariness * in the face of the insoluble Congo problem, and his grief at being called a murderer. He had always known that the great trial would come—and now it was here. On 6 July 1961 he wrote this poem, inspired by his mountain-climbing:

> Tired
> And lonely,
> So tired
> The heart aches.
> Meltwater trickles
> Down the rocks,
> The fingers are numb,
> The knees tremble.
> It is now,
> Now, that you must not give in.

* How pessimistic was Hammarskjöld's view of the world situation appears in a letter written when his friend, the great Swedish writer Hjalmar Gullberg, had just died:

"Not for a very long time has news of a death seemed so grievous to a Swede of our generation. He was one of the few, and perhaps last, representatives of a lofty spirit, with natural dignity, a warm heart and unshakable integrity, who are needed more than ever in this time of growing darkness and corruption."

On the path of the others
Are resting places,
Places in the sun
Where they can meet.
But this
Is your path,
And it is now,
Now, that you must not fail.

Weep
If you can,
Weep,
But do not complain.
The way chose you—
And you must be thankful.

A
Spiritual
Portrait

Now no will-power could help him, no heroism. He felt how his finest achievement was made
the object of the most brutal abuse. Perhaps it too
would fail? And afterwards?

Thou
Whom I do not know
But Whose I am.
Thou
Whom I do not comprehend
But Who hast dedicated me
To my fate.
Thou—

In the late night hours he would lie brooding, wondering whether he had done the right thing, and why he acted as he did. And he found no answer. Death lured him with its release from all pressures. On 3 December, 1960, he had gathered his whole experience in a poem which all the children in the Sweden of the future will be learning by heart.

> The road,
> You shall follow it.
>
> The fun,
> You shall forget it.
>
> The cup,
> You shall empty it.
>
> The pain,
> You shall conceal it.
>
> The truth,
> You shall be told it.
>
> The end,
> You shall endure it.

The end—you shall endure it.
Everyone knows how the end came. In a last,

desperate effort Hammarskjöld was willing to stake everything to put an end at last to the bloody conflict in the Congo. When, pale and with dark shadows under his eyes, he said goodbye to his friend and colleague Sture Linnér at the airport, he had in his pocket Thomas à Kempis' *Imitation of Christ*, which he quotes so often in his diary and which towards the end of his life lay on his bedside table in New York. The only thing he then talked of was—love.

On 26 November 1960 he had written a poem about Christ:

The moon was caught in the branches:
Bound by its vow,
My heart was heavy.

Naked against the night
The trees slept. "Nevertheless,
Not as I will. . . ."

The burden remained mine:
They could not hear my call,
And all was silence.

Soon, now, the torches, the kiss:
Soon the gray of dawn
In the Judgment Hall.

What will their love help there?
There, the question is only
If I love them.

This is certainly a poem about the Saviour; but
there are lines in it which one cannot read without thinking of his disciple Hammarskjöld:

> The burden remained mine:
> They could not hear my call,
> And all was silence.

> There, the question is only
> If I love them . . .

We do not know whether Hammarskjöld's
plane was shot down by his enemies in the
Congo; it seems probable. So he was killed perhaps by the very people he loved and came to
save.

If he was able to collect himself to think a
thought or make a prayer, flung from the plane
and sitting alone on the ground in that far country, we may suppose that this was what was in
his mind.

At Whitsun 1961 he had written:

"I don't know Who—or what—put the question, I don't know when it was put. I don't even

remember answering. But at some moment I did answer *Yes* to Someone—or Something—and from that hour I was certain that existence is meaningful and that, therefore, my life, in self-surrender, had a goal."

He says in the same context that he was brought forward to a point where he saw that his way must lead to a "triumph which is a catastrophe, and to a catastrophe which is a triumph, that the price for committing one's life would be reproach, and that the only elevation possible to man lies in the depths of humiliation."

The humiliation was there: the world turned against him in suspicion and contempt: the solution of the Congo struggle seemed to be slipping from his grasp.

And death was approaching.